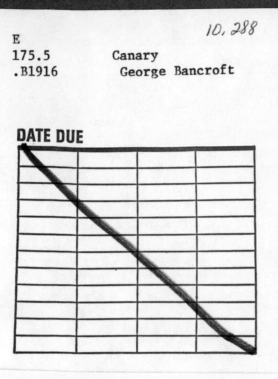

DATE DUE

Twayne's United States Authors Series

Sylvia E. Bowman, *Editor*
INDIANA UNIVERSITY

George Bancroft

GEORGE BANCROFT

By ROBERT H. CANARY

University of Wisconsin–Parkside

 266

Twayne Publishers, Inc.   ::   New York

ISBN 0-8057-0034-X
MANUFACTURED IN THE UNITED STATES OF AMERICA

For Marjorie, Margaret, and Linda Canary

Preface

GEORGE BANCROFT (1800-1891) was one of the first great American historians and one of the most widely read American historical writers of his time. He combined his work as a historian with a distinguished career in politics and diplomacy. To both careers he brought a breadth of vision which makes his *History of the United States* (1834-1885) a literary as well as a historical achievement. Although he is no longer much read by the general public, Bancroft's work remains important for historians, for he helped establish the framework within which we see our early history. Although more recent historians have challenged almost every significant point of interpretation in the *History*, Bancroft helped set the terms for the debate. But he is not simply an honored predecessor, since he can still be read with profit by the specialist. Later scholars have done even more intensive research on many points and have often been more scrupulous in their documentation, but Bancroft had a mastery of the facts rarely if ever equaled since. His great value depends on his success in marshaling these facts into a coherent narrative synthesis of early American history. This synthesis demands continued attention since, by giving form, it gives meaning to the chaos of history.

More widely read than his most talented contemporaries who wrote fiction, Bancroft would be of interest to the literary and cultural historian even if his histories were no more reliable than Parson Weems's biography of George Washington. As one whose intensive exploration of the sources and mastery of detail produced histories still worthy of professional respect, he would be of interest to the historiographer were he no more readable than, say Hubert Howe Bancroft. But George Bancroft mastered the skills of both the artist and the scholar; like his contemporaries, William Prescott and Francis Parkman, he was one of America's great "literary" historians. This study is an attempt to illuminate the literary dimensions of his dual achievement. It argues that Bancroft's literary success was a result of his ability to produce a narrative synthesis of events, that the methods and effects of narrative history resemble those of other narratives, and that narrative form and manner are not one thing in history and another in literary genres. This study offers itself, then, as a contribution to the current discussion of the nature of narrative as well as an attempt to define the specific achievement of Bancroft.

I have chosen to concentrate on *The History of the United States from the Discovery of the Continent*. No other choice is really possible. Originally published in ten volumes (1834-1875), the *History* was revised and condensed for the six-volume Centenary Edition (1876-79). Two volumes on the *History of the Formation of the Constitution of the United States of America* (1882) were originally published separately, but they became a part of the larger *History* in the six-volume *Author's Last Revision* (1883-85). In effect, Bancroft devoted his professional life to one major work. Nothing else he wrote approaches it in interest and importance; in fact, it is doubtful whether any of his minor works qualifies as literature at all, and they have been dealt with very briefly in this study. Dealing with a work published piecemeal over a period of time poses some special problems, for the work's unity is cumulative. I have chosen to begin by treating the first volume of the *History* as a work complete in itself. Thereafter, the units of the *History* which deal with periods of history are discussed in the order of their appearance in print. I end by considering the *History* as a completed whole.

Concentrating on analysis of the *History* means that less attention is given to Bancroft's public career. The biographical portions of this study are placed where they will cast light on the literary issues being considered. Bancroft's early life is discussed in Chapter 1, in connection with his philosophy of history and the first volume of the *History*. Chapter 2 deals with the political implications of the first unit of the *History*, and it includes a section discussing his political career up to about 1845. His later public career and his friendships with other historians are discussed in Chapter 6, where they can contribute to our assessment of Bancroft as a man and a historian. Useful biographies are available for readers wishing additional details. I have necessarily relied on them myself, but I have tried to read the sources for myself, and I believe this study makes a few new points and cites some new evidence, even in the biographical sections.

Although Bancroft's life and work are taken up in roughly chronological order, each chapter takes up a different literary and historiographical issue. The first two chapters deal with the philosophic and political predispositions which helped determine the form and meaning of the *History*. Chapter 3 discusses the formal unity of the *History* as a product of the careful subordination of materials to a plot composed of interdependent lines of action linking together certain essential incidents. Chapter 4 includes an examination of Bancroft's construction of episodes and some remarks on his narrative voice, the distinguishing mark of narrative as a manner of presentation. Chapter 5 brings the level of analysis down to stylistic detail with a discussion of Bancroft's revisions and a discussion of historical explanation. Chapter 6 discusses the purposes and satisfactions of historical writing, and attempts to evaluate the *History* as literature. A brief concluding chapter summarizes the argument for Bancroft as an important figure in American literary history.

The critical approach adopted is eclectic; but, since Bancroft's strength as a historian is in narrative construction, I have naturally been drawn to critical approaches which emphasize structure rather than style. I have also been much influenced by the current philosophical debate over the nature of historical narrative. Readers familar with this debate will recognize my position as that of an unreconstructed "narrativist," although I have tried to avoid theoretical digressions. Some of the issues involved are relevant to our appreciation of Bancroft, and these are touched on briefly in Chapters 5 and 6; at other points, the relevant philosophic discussions are simply cited in the Notes and References. I believe that many of the points raised by the debate over historical explanation are relevant to the critical discussion of narrative in general.

Research for this study was partially supported by grants from the San Diego State Foundation and from the University of Hawaii. I am also grateful to the University of Wisconsin-Parkside for its support of *CLIO: An Interdisciplinary Journal of Literature, History, and the Philosophy of History*, for my service as coeditor of that journal has done much to sharpen my thinking on the questions raised by this study. Manuscript collections examined include the American Antiquarian Society, the University of California at Berkeley, Cornell University (on microfilm), the Huntington Library, the Library of Congress, the Massachusetts Historical Society, the New York Public

Library, and Stanford University, leaving me in debt to a score of helpful librarians. Of those who have made helpful comments on this manuscript, I can mention only Margaret Canary, David Fong, Hedi St. Denis, and my editor, Sylvia E. Bowman.

ROBERT H. CANARY

University of Wisconsin-Parkside

Contents

Chronology

1800	George Bancroft born in Worcester, Massachusetts, October 3.
1811	Enters Phillips Academy, Exeter, New Hampshire.
1813	Enters Harvard College.
1818	Sets sail June 27 for Europe to pursue theological studies.
1820	Receives Doctor of Philosophy degree from University of Göttingen, September 9.
1822	Returns to Cambridge, Massachusetts, August 8. Serves Harvard as a tutor in Greek.
1823	Publishes *Poems* and first article in *North American Review*. Joins with Joseph Cogswell to establish Round Hill School, Northampton, Massachusetts.
1826	Gives Fourth of July oration at Northampton, launching political career.
1827	Marries Sarah Dwight.
1831	Leaves Round Hill School, September 1, to devote time to writing and to the Dwight business interests.
1834	Publishes Volume I of *History of the United States*. Nominated by Anti-Masons for Massachusetts General Court. Loses but out-polls Democratic nominee.
1836	Formally joins Democratic party. Runs and loses as a Democratic candidate for Congress.
1837	Publishes Volume II of *History of the United States*. Wife Sarah dies.
1938	Becomes Collector of the Port of Boston. Moves to Boston. Marries Elizabeth Davis Bliss.
1839	Publishes Volume III of *History of the United States*.
1840	Loses collectorship.
1844	Helps arrange J. K. Polk's nomination for President. Runs unsuccessfully for governor of Massachusetts.
1845	Becomes Secretary of the Navy. Moves to Washington. Serves for a time as Acting Secretary of War.

1846   Becomes United States Minister to London. Sails for London, October 10.

1849   Dismissed from post. Returns to reside in New York City.

1852   Publishes Volumes IV and V of *History of the United States*.

1855   Publishes *Literary and Historical Miscellanies*.

1856   Publishes Volume VI of *History of the United States*.

1858   Publishes Volume VII of *History of the United States*.

1860   Publishes Volume VIII of *History of the United States*.

1864   As a War Democrat, supports Abraham Lincoln for President.

1865   Secretly drafts Andrew Johnson's first message to Congress.

1866   Delivers memorial oration on Lincoln to joint session of Congress. Publishes Volume IX of *History of the United States*.

1867   Engaged in public controversy with descendants of men dealt with in Volume IX. Publishes *Joseph Reed*. Becomes United States Minister to Prussia. Sails for Berlin, July 10.

1873   Resigns post.

1874   Returns to settle in Washington, D.C. Publishes Volume X of *History of the United States*.

1875–   Publishes revised Centenary Edition of *History of the United*
1876   *States*.(six volumes).

1882   Publishes *The History of the Formation of the Federal Constitution* (two volumes).

1883   Publishes *A Plea for the Constitution of the United States; Wounded in the House of its Guardians*.

1883–   Publishes "The Author's Last Revision" of the *History of the*
1885   *United States*.

1886   Addresses annual meeting of American Historical Association.

1887   Projects a biography of J. K. Polk.

1888   Publishes *Martin Van Buren*.

1891   Dies in Washington, D.C., January 17; buried in Worcester.

CHAPTER I

The Historian and History

O N April 27, 1886, GEORGE BANCROFT took the chair of the third annual meeting of the American Historical Association and delivered his presidential address. Many in his audience had not yet been born in 1834 when the first volume of Bancroft's *History of the United States from the Discovery of the Continent* had made him famous almost overnight. Now in his eighties, Bancroft was still vigorous and had just completed a six-volume "Author's Last Revision" of his monumental history. But the kind of history Bancroft wrote was already out of fashion—if not with the public, certainly with the professional, academic historians in his audience. The warmest tribute to Bancroft at the meeting came in a letter from an old friend, the great German historian Leopold von Ranke. Accepting an honorary membership in the fledgling association, Ranke, another patriarch of the profession, five years older than Bancroft, expressed "especial joy to see Mr. George Bancroft, one of the masters in our science, extending his hand to me from afar."[1]

The presidency of the association was itself a tribute to Bancroft from a younger generation that was often critical of his methods and conclusions. To Bancroft, it was one of the last honors received in a lifetime of honors earned. Bancroft had been Secretary of the Navy in President James K. Polk's cabinet; he had represented the United States at the courts of England and Germany; he had delivered the memorial eulogy of Abraham Lincoln to a joint session of Congress, had written Andrew Johnson's first message to Congress, and then had given the official eulogy of Johnson. Holding no public office, advancing no special interests, and backed by no political or economic power group, Bancroft had been granted free access to the floor of the United States Senate. Had he left his history incomplete years before, he would still have had a place in history as the man responsible for establishing the Naval Academy at Annapolis.

But the presidency of the American Historical Association had a special meaning for George Bancroft because his long public career had never interfered for long with his devotion to the Muse of history; indeed, much of his public career was based in part on his fame as a historian. He had befriended many young historians and passed on material to others. At the end of this meeting he politely assured those who read papers "that he never had listened to a series of papers so interesting, so thorough, so accurate, and so instructive."[2] In his presidential address, he spelled out for the audience his own philosophy of history, views which he had acquired early in his career, which reflected his own early training, and which are exemplified in his history as early as his first volume of 1834.

I   *The "Science" of History*

History, Bancroft told his colleagues, has "the character of science.... The movements of mankind are governed by law," and the task of the historian is "discerning the presence of law" in the events of history.[3] Thus far, few of Bancroft's hearers would have disagreed with him. But many of those who joined with him in coveting the name of "science" could not accept his implicit definition. For them, science meant rigor, precision, objectivity; and Bancroft seemed to have none of these. Bancroft's historical "science" was "nearest of kin to the students of moral philosophy" (550). The laws that he found in history were more like working hypotheses or models, useful to the extent that they might help order large masses of data; but they were too vague to seem really "scientific." Bancroft all too obviously brought his "laws" with him when he came to examine history; they were part of his basic assumptions about the nature of man and the world he lived in.

In support of his description of their common pursuit, Bancroft offered his hearers a series of observations on the American experience of self-government. This "government by all" is a special blessing since "A government that is less than government by an entire people will by its very nature incline to the benefit of the classes" (551). This democratic literalism is also invoked to explain the preservation of the Union in the Civil War: "The will of the people was able to exact its preservation" (551). For Bancroft, the directions taken by this self-governing nation exemplify the workings of the laws of his history. In those days of innocence, Bancroft could claim that "The United States have never importuned or encouraged others to adopt their principles of government prematurely" (552) and could "explain" this statement by citing Montesquieu's notion that "the spirit of a republic is peace and moderation." The difficulty of amending the Constitution is explained, not in terms of the conservatism of its authors but in those of the democratic ideal: "A Constitution may be changed only after a reference in some form to every individual in the community" (553).

"On Self Government" thus presents in capsule form some of the leading ideas of Bancroft's *History*. Just as he believes in the democratic ideal so does he believe that history proves its value and viability: "This government by the people and for the people is the oldest one now existing in the civilized world this side of the empire of the Czars" (553). He is by no means a radical—Americans are the "most conservative" people in the world (552)—but he believes that the course of history is and must be determined by the will of the people. Since the will of the people is just, as well as inevitable, history also demonstrates the moral progress of the race. This point, too, is touched on in "On Self-Government": Bancroft surveys with satisfaction the introduction of republics in France and Switzerland and particularly the new ascendency of the House of Commons in Great Britain. Although the end of the republic of Holland and one or two other pieces of contrary evidence are noted, the implication seems to be that self-government is the wave of the future.

A clearer statement of Bancroft's belief in progress and of its implications for the historian may be found in a speech given in 1854, "The Necessity, The Reality and The Promise of the Progress of the Human Race."[4] In it, we also find a radical assertion of the essential equality of man: "Every man is in substance equal to his fellow man" (483). No country can progress much farther than the collective genius of its people will allow; and, if the new age brings forth no Plato, no Raphael, or no Kant, progress will be assured since the mass of men are ever growing better and wiser. As man grows wiser, he will inevitably discern the benefits of democratic institutions; and one day all "political institutions will rest on the basis of equality and freedom" (514). Reformers cannot force this process from above, nor can revolutions create it by upheaval; it must wait upon the evolving wisdom of the race, and then "All the despotisms on earth cannot stay its coming" (515). This insistence that change could not be forced enabled Bancroft to oppose all political changes he disliked as inevitably ineffective while supporting others as the will of history. As in "On Self-Government," Bancroft here links his democratic idealism to American patriotism; America embodies the coming unity of the human race—it "is bound to allure the world to freedom by the beauty of its example" (516).

In this 1854 oration, Bancroft speaks again of laws and of science, but he makes it clear that they represent the progressive efforts of mankind to know a truth which is conceived of as both absolute and ideal. The very "necessity" of progress arises from the existence of this unrealized ideal truth. The ideal man and the ideal state are absolutes, and our moral duty is to struggle to realize them. History and the historian fairly judge the statesman by his willingness "to make every advancement that the culture of his time will sustain" (487), "to raise the world from the actual toward the ideal" (488). Bancroft's law of progress thus provides a criterion for judgment as well as an explanation of history. It enables him to see himself as speaking for the race in praising progressive politicians and in condemning those who seem to him to speak for the selfish interests of particular classes.

Bancroft has no doubt that this necessary progress is indeed a "reality." The evidence he advances to prove his point is largely drawn from the material progress of civilization, despite his rhetorical attacks on materialists and atheists. He cites advances in various sciences and in mechanical inventions such as steam navigation, canals and railroads, electricity. Speaking in the North, he refers to "mighty strides toward the abolition of servitude," although he makes no direct reference to the American South. He acknowledges that women are now seemingly barred from public life, but he urges that they have obtained "the uniform enjoyment of domestic equality." Remarks like this one provide stronger evidence for Bancroft's optimism than for his thesis—and the same comment may perhaps be made on his view of the "promise" of mankind's moral progress—the promise of unity, universality, and freedom for the race. The twentieth century, reading the great nineteenth-century American historians, has come to prefer Parkman and Prescott, men with a darker view of history.

Bancroft's view of the future of the race can be optimistic because he sees progress as both the law of history and the will of God. History is in the hands of Providence, and the historian's task is to reveal and justify God's ways to man: "It is because God is visible in History that his office is noblest except that of the poet" (492). Bancroft's father helped found the American Unitarian Association, but Bancroft speaks here of "the triune God" (504) and condemns Arianism. His notion of history as controlled by God's providence also seems to go back beyond the relatively rationalistic Unitarians, for the New England Puritans in particular had seen God in each event of history and had ascribed to Him a special interest in His children in America. Whatever the source of his ideas, Bancroft makes it clear in this address that his sense of America's special mission in history is based on a belief that it is in some way an instrument of Providence.[5]

An oration delivered in 1835, "The Office of the People in Art, Government, and Religion," connects the providential theory of the 1854 address with the faith in common men found in "On Self-Government" and states both even more strongly.[6] "Providence never disowns the race" (434). The Spirit in man is God-given, and so mankind cannot help but progress: "It is the uniform tendency of the popular element to elevate and bless Humanity. The exact measure of the progress of civilization is the degree to which the intelligence of the common mind has prevailed over wealth and brute force; in other words, the measure of the progress of civilization is the progress of the people" (426-27). In art, government, and religion, then, the will of the people must and will prevail.

Such were Bancroft's beliefs about the nature of history and the duty of the historian. He held to them more or less consistently all his life and gave them frequent expression. They are of importance because in the *History* these oratorical statements become unifying themes. In the early books of the *History* his views are especially apparent, for the oratory sometimes spills over into the book, forcing the reader to listen to speeches while reading the histories. In later volumes and in revisions, Bancroft reduced the frequency of these oratorical flourishes, but his address to the American Historical Association shows that he had not changed his mind on any fundamental point.

It is not surprising, then, to find these views expressed in the Introduction to the first volume of the *History* and in its Preface. The latter introduces the theme elaborated on in "On Self-Government" some fifty years later: "The spirit of the colonies demanded freedom from the beginning. It was in this period, that Virginia first asserted the doctrine of popular sovereignty; that the people of Maryland constituted their own government; that New Plymouth, Connecticut, New Haven, New Hampshire, Maine, rested their legislation on the popular will; that Massachusetts declared itself a perfect commonwealth."[7]

The Introduction parallels the wonders Bancroft was to cite to prove the reality of progress in 1854 with a similar list of those available in 1834, which are used to prove the greatness of the achievement of the United States. Bancroft tells us that his history's task will be to show

how this progress has come about, but his answer is implicit in the phrasing of the question: "It is the object of the present work to explain how the change in the condition of our land has been accomplished; and, as the fortunes of the nation are not under the control of blind destiny, to follow the steps by which a favoring Providence, calling our institutions into being, has conducted the country to its present happiness and glory" (4).

The Preface also sets forth Bancroft's methodology. He has sought to rely on authentic documents, applying to them and to all witnesses "the principles of historical skepticism" (v). He has done his best to find and examine the reports of all nations, factions, of individuals involved in important incidents. These principles seem unexceptional today, but Bancroft was not being entirely unfair in claiming that many of his predecessors, "where materials were not at hand, substituted the inferences of the writer for authenticated facts" (vi). Bancroft's own use of his sources was not always as scrupulous as some of his successors have thought proper. But when the younger historians of the American Historical Association honored Bancroft, they were recognizing that, despite his patriotic idealism, he had rarely compromised "the sincerity with which I have sought to collect truth from trust-worthy documents and testimony" (v). For the source of Bancroft's views, both those that they accepted and those that they rejected, we must turn to Bancroft's life prior to 1834—the years which formed him as a historian and as a man.

II   *The Making of a Historian*

Many of Bancroft's views can be traced to influences operating on him in his formative years: his family background, his study for the ministry, his academic training in Germany, and his literary ambitions.[8] It was recognized early that Bancroft was gifted beyond the average, and great expectations were held for him. Although about as modest as a bright young man can be expected to be, Bancroft was ambitious enough to share those expectations. It seemed at first that he would fall far short, but the *History* vindicated the hopes of his family and friends.

His father, Aaron Bancroft, had a brave and successful career, one which Bancroft may at times have despaired of equaling. The Bancrofts had been respectable farmers since coming to America in 1632, but Aaron Bancroft supplemented the curriculum of his common school with private study and was able to enter Harvard in 1774, when he was not quite nineteen, rather old for an entering student at the time. After graduation in 1778, he accepted in 1780 a Congregational mission to Nova Scotia, where he stayed three years. In 1783, he was called back to Massachusetts as a substitute for the pastor of Old South Church in Worcester. His liberal views so shocked the majority of his congregation that the church did not follow custom by appointing him successor when the pastor died. However, sixty-seven dissidents who left the church and formed the Second Congregational Church of Worcester called Aaron Bancroft as their minister. It was a lonely fight. For the first few years Bancroft's parishioners were still required by law to support the Old South Church; for seven years, no other church in Massachusetts invited him to exchange pulpits for a Sunday; and many of his fellow clergymen regarded him as a heretic. But he won: in 1792 his new church erected its permanent meeting-house; his salary, at first so low that he had to eke out a livelihood by doubling as a tutor in Greek and Latin, was raised to respectable sums in the new century.

By the time his son George came of age, Aaron Bancroft was recognized as one of the leading clergymen of Massachusetts. His writings had helped win him this admiration and respect, and none more so than his *Life of Washington* (1807). Based primarily on the works of others, like John Marshall's just-completed five-volume study, Aaron's biography was more readable than Marshall, more reliable than Weems, and justly popular. The next few years saw the triumph of religious liberalism in Massachusetts; in 1825, Aaron Bancroft was one of the founders of the American Unitarian Association and its honorary president. When he died in 1839, he had had the additional satisfaction of seeing the outlines of his son's success. In old age, when asked whether he would be willing to live his life over again, he always answered that he would.

As a substitute in the pulpit of Old South Church, Aaron Bancroft had startled the congregation by proclaiming the primacy of reason, the harmony of reason and revelation, and the consequent need to reject what claimed to be revealed yet could not be harmonized with reason. The rationalism that was part of his religion was a part of his character as well. Late in life he wrote his "Memoranda designed for the Inspection of my Wife and my Children," but even in it he says little about his religious beliefs and practices: "Possibly in these things I have been thro' life too reserved; but my heart always revolted from communications of this nature. Religion, as a concern between God and the soul of man, is in its essence a secret transaction, and not to be spoken of to the world."[9] Some time after his father's death George Bancroft remembered him as one who did not "make a show of his virtues or his emotions. ... His affections were strong, but not demonstrative."[10] Aaron Bancroft's wife Lucretia, daughter of a Tory family which had lost everything it had in the Revolution, was evidently warmer and gayer than her husband; but she was an uneducated woman whose life was centered on her husband. Life in the Bancroft household was determined by the gentle, austere nature of Aaron Bancroft; and it was by his high standards that George Bancroft first sought to measure himself.

George Bancroft later rejected rationalism in religion and stressed his father's closeness to conservative religious views. But one product of his father's rationalistic temperament was a habitual suspension of judgment which provided a healthy model for the future historian. At Aaron's funeral, the minister spoke of an incident which had occurred during the great struggle between the new liberalists in religion and adherents of older views. When his daughter Eliza asked if she could read his friend Channing's letters to Dr. Worchester, he asked if she had read Dr. Worchester's Letters; and, when she admitted that she had not "with some expression of disparagement," her father said: "What, are you a daughter of mine, and do you read only one side of the question?"[11] He rarely gave his opinion on religious disputes to his children, insisting that they investigate and form their own opinions; his son could not "recall a single instance in which he attempted to mould or sway my opinions on religious dogmas or politics."[12] When George Bancroft spoke, in the Preface to his first volume, of reading the reports of both parties to a conflict, he was speaking of lessons learned long before he encountered history as a discipline.

Harvard gave his father an honorary doctorate in divinity in 1810, and it was to Harvard that George Bancroft went in 1813. After two years of excellent training at Phillips Academy in Exeter, he had passed his college entrance examination at the age of thirteen. At Harvard, his closest friendships were with the faculty rather than with his fellow students. Andrew Norton, the "Unitarian Pope," was a friend of his father and befriended Bancroft; President Kirkland received him many evenings; and he came to know well his Latin tutor, Edward Everett. These three men were perhaps the most stimulating figures at Harvard in Bancroft's era. All Unitarian ministers as well as scholars, they urged Bancroft to follow his father's path from Harvard into the ministry, and Bancroft was willing. It seems curious, then, that he should at this time develop an enthusiasm for the Calvinist writings of Jonathan Edwards, but Norton's relatively conservative Unitarianism may have been a factor. In any event, Bancroft's senior-year essay on "The Use and Necessity of Revelation" offers a theology much less liberal than that of Aaron Bancroft; the essay stresses the weakness of mankind and the inadequacy of reason.

Edward Everett, who had studied the classics in Germany, sang the praises of German scholarship to Bancroft. President Kirkland, anxious to have some of his outstanding scholars improve themselves abroad, helped secure funds from the Harvard Overseers and other sources to supplement what Bancroft's family could raise; and in June, 1818, George Bancroft embarked for Germany. The hope was that he might prepare himself for the ministry; indeed, the money granted by the Overseers was for him to "pursue his theological studies," and President Kirkland wrote, in a letter of introduction to a German scholar, "They wish him to attend especially to philology, the ancient languages and Oriental literature, that he may thus be qualified to pursue theological studies to the greatest benefit, to give instruction as any opening may occur and invite, and become an accomplished philologian and biblical critic, able to expound and defend the Revelation of God."[13]

Carrying introductory letters from Kirkland and Everett, possessing the natural advantages of youth, and representing a new land still of great interest to Europeans, Bancroft had no difficulty in making acquaintances in Germany and elsewhere on the Continent. His own hard work and genuine intelligence won him many friends, as well as a doctorate from Göttingen in 1820. Yet his letters home from Göttingen and Berlin, where he spent his first winter, often express a provincial's distrust of the Continent's social sophistication and religious skepticism. The more he absorbed of European theology, the more Bancroft wondered whether his new learning would be well-received in America: "Who would to dare to interpret in America the epistles to the Hebrews, the Apocalypse, but above all the O.T. as it must and ought to be done? The cry of heresy will attend the first attempt."[14] Although he continued to assume that he would become a minister on his return, he worried that nothing he could do in America would bring him lasting fame. He wrote his father that he might prefer a New York City pulpit—"I should never wish to become a clergyman in Boston."[15] He allowed himself to drift away from a strict concentration on theological and philological studies and attended lectures on history and education. He began to read widely in European literature, treasured his meetings with literary lions like Lord Byron and Goethe, and wrote much verse himself.

Almost in spite of himself, Bancroft became a man of the world; and, although his familiarity with Continental manners later helped him in his diplomatic career, his Harvard friends were dismayed to find that their earnest young acolyte had returned after four years in Europe as a bearded dandy. When Bancroft greeted Andrew Norton with the Continental kiss upon each cheek, the deeply offended Norton broke off their relationship; and they did not speak to each other for six years. With no immediate opening in the ministry, Bancroft undertook to repay Harvard its investment in him by serving as a tutor in Greek for the academic year 1822-23. The students, like some of his colleagues, disliked and laughed at his Germanophilia and his Continental mannerisms. As Aaron Bancroft's son, he was frequently invited to visit in various Massachusetts pulpits; but, despite his good intentions, his sermons struck many of their hearers as overly ornate and pedantic. Bancroft recognized his failure and decided to forswear a ministerial career. Less than a year after Bancroft's return, Emerson would write in his journal that "He hath sadly disappointed great expectations, and for the present hath done preaching."[16]

Having discovered his lack of vocation for the clerical life, Bancroft was now to make education his career. In Germany, he had been more favorably impressed with the German *gymnasium* than with the German university. After his first year abroad, when he wrote Edward Everett claiming that some Boston gentlemen had suggested that he might set up a high school on those lines in America, Bancroft asked Everett's opinion but was careful not to sound personally enthusiastic: "The labor of a school is nothing alluring; but it must be confessed, this would be the way of doing most good. . . . I should be too young to begin anything, that would decide my destiny for life, and could perhaps for five years do nought better than attempt to establish a learned school."[17] At Berlin, he had attended Friedrich Schleiermacher's lectures on educational theory and made the friendship of the lecturer. He had visited the famous school at Schulfuria and outlined in his journal the rules for the sort of school he proposed.

It was natural that Bancroft should attempt to establish such a school when it became clear that the ministry was not for him and that he was not happy at Harvard. Although his Harvard students learned more than ever before, it was against their will; and he was no more popular with the faculty than with the students. Bancroft wanted to reform the college, but he lacked the patience to seek change in the tedious ways even then characteristic of American higher education. Most of his colleagues thought him arrogant; among the few who understood were two others who had studied abroad, George Ticknor and Joseph Cogswell. Cogswell, the college librarian, decided to join with Bancroft in founding a new school. Together they secured a site near Northampton, Massachusetts, and prepared to open for classes in the fall of 1823.

Round Hill School opened that fall with three faculty members and twenty-five students; in a few years it had a dozen instructors and over a hundred students. The organization of the school reflected much of what Bancroft and Cogswell had heard and seen in Europe. There was no corporal punishment, and Cogswell in particular cultivated a camaraderie with the boys. Students were encouraged to work at their own pace, the curriculum was broad, the faculty more than competent, and the work was intensive. The boy who graduated from Round Hill was well-prepared for college, far better prepared than the colleges of the time required for entrance. A success in every way except the financial, the school finally expired some three years after Bancroft left it in 1831.

Bancroft had begun by being happy at Round Hill, for it seemd to offer a congenial combination of "retirement and employment. I love them both. ... The principles which we believed to be well-founded, and which so many esteemed visionary, are in fact perfectly just and practical. Anything may be done with an uncorrupted mind."[18] But long before he had left the school and had sold his share to Cogswell, he had grown restive, unhappy "that my early manhood should be employed in restraining the petulance and assisting the weakness of children, when I am conscious of sufficient courage to sustain collisions with men."[19] Such thoughts surely occur to most teachers at one time or another, but Bancroft seems to have been, from the first, gifted with the temperament of a scholar rather than with the ability of a teacher. A former pupil later recalled that Bancroft, like many later scholars, "seemed to be more earnestly bent on learning for himself than on helping them to learn."[20] Bancroft's marriage to Sarah Dwight in 1827 may have helped him bear his life at Round Hill a while longer; the approaching birth of his first child may have hastened his departure.

Sarah Dwight came from Springfield, Massachusetts; and Bancroft had met her when she had visited Northhampton. In March, 1826, he wrote her proposing marriage; she replied that short acquaintance had left her unprepared to decide quickly, and she was still unwilling after three weeks of consideration to have the engagement made public.[21] Even then, it was nearly a year before they were married, a wait which Bancroft endured with a becoming lack of patience—"I will not even pretend an indifference to the pleasures which are in prospect."[22] The marriage had the advantage of securing Bancroft's financial future; the Dwights were a large family of wealthy businessmen. When Bancroft left Round Hill, he had sufficient savings to provide for a year or so of retirement; he could add to this sum by undertaking occasional missions for the Dwight family enterprises. But the marriage seems to have been a true love match; in Bancroft's correspondence, his letters to his wife form a pleasant contrast to the business correspondence demanded by his new duties.[23] Nor did he plan to make his business career permanent: "collisions with men" he might get aplenty in the business world, but not that idealistic justification which, as his father's son, he craved. By the time he left Round Hill, Bancroft was already embarked on the two careers, history and politics, that were ultimately to gratify his desire to win fame by doing good—an ambition instilled in him early in life and frustrated in the years immediately following his return to America.

III   *Apprenticeship*

Bancroft thought to make himself known as a man of letters long before the publication of the *History*, and his first effort in this direction was the publication of *Poems* in 1823—carefully revised versions of verses he had scribbled while in Europe. In them, Bancroft reflected his youthful enthusiasm for the role of the poet and for the poets he had read and admired while in Europe—Lord Byron, Sir Walter Scott, Friedrich von Schiller, and other Romantics. The poems do not reflect any special talent for poetry, and the volume was generally ignored. Chastened by this neglect, Bancroft concluded that he had the diligence required of a scholar rather than the inventiveness required of a poet. In later years he tried to buy up all extant copies to have them destroyed. Had he succeeded, we might have thought the volume contained some youthful indiscretions; but we can now attribute this effort to his improved literary taste.[24]

Although a complete failure as a poet, Bancroft was more successful in making a name for himself as a promising young critic. In October, 1823, he published his first effort in this line, a note on "Schiller's Minor Poems" for the prestigious *North American Review*. In the years before the appearance of the *History*, Bancroft published about two dozen articles and reviews. Most of them appeared in the *North American*, but an important series on German literature appeared in 1827 and 1828 in Robert Walsh's *American Quarterly Review*. Articles on Schiller, Goethe, and Herder for the *North American* had given Bancroft a reputation for special expertise in German history and literature, and his articles in the *American Quarterly* confirmed this.[25] Edward Everett, a former editor of the *North American*, wrote its current editor, Jared Sparks, "it is absolutely necessary, I think, to win back Bancroft. He wrote by far the best piece in Walsh's last—You must pardon me for saying you *must* pay as much as Walsh."[26] Bancroft was soon, however, to shift his focus from literary criticism to politics, but his literary articles had helped win him an audience and a name. In 1855 he still thought well enough of some of his early material to revise and reprint it as "Studies in German Literature" in the *Miscellanies.*

If the subject matter of many of these pieces was drawn from his sojourn abroad, the style was unfortunately like the sermons he had delivered on his return. Even in an age of heavily rhetorical prose, Bancroft's style struck some as affected. A troublesome contributor in many ways, Bancroft resisted editorial revisions and objected strongly when they were made in the printed copy. The historian-editor Sparks wrote Bancroft that his two great errors were, "first, to suffer yourself to be unduly excited about comparatively small things; and secondly, to have little respect for the judgment of others." In a second letter, the exasperated Sparks made his point with a force he rarely showed in his work as a historian: "I believe there is no mortal whose views on this subject in any respect resemble yours, and if all writers were thus minded, an editor's condition would be very much like that of a toad under a harrow. No man, in fact, would stand to such a post long—but let that pass."[27] Everett, who knew them both, felt that Bancroft was "not without reason" in rebelling against Sparks' editorial practice.[28] When unauthorized emendations were made in Bancroft's political articles, he ended his association with the *North American*.

Bancroft's view of the literary artist resembles his view of the historian. He sees both poetry and history in cultural terms, where we are apt to see poetry as an individual product and history as a disciplinary ideal; he believes in the moral responsibility of both the poet and the historian, where we believe, or say we do, in the amorality of art and the objectivity of the historical ideal. Bancroft's poet may act under inspiration, but he is not to act freely: he must teach men to elevate their minds and to restrain their passions, but he is also to give them pleasure. Learning and letters in Germany are seen as conditioned by the historical setting. Poets, like statesmen, participate in the progress of history; their art will fail them if they swerve from the true course: "The speculative tendency of Schiller's mind led him to make an experiment of introducing the Greek chorus into modern tragedy. The experiment failed, and the Bride of Messalina is sustained by the splendor of its several parts, not by its general merits. The poet returned at once to the right path, and history again lent itself to his genius" (*Miscellanies*, 184-85).

Like statesmen, poets may be judged by their allegiance to political progress; in the same passage, Schiller is praised for his "love of humanity . . . zeal for freedom and social progress" (*Miscellanies*, 185). It is easy to see why Bancroft found it easy to move from would-be poet to critic to historian; to him, the task of each was similar.

Literary ambitions were by no means the only spurs to writing in this period, for the founders of Round Hill soon found existing textbooks unsatisfactory for their new enterprise. Bancroft therefore translated several textbooks from the German for use at the school: a Greek grammar, a Latin reader, and an edition of Cornelius Nepos were published between 1824 and 1826; and in 1829 he revised a previous translation of a Latin grammar. Like, perhaps, Round Hill itself, these works are of more interest for the introduction of Germanic influence in American education than in themselves. Much more important for Bancroft's own development were his translations from the German of works by his history professor at Göttingen, August Heeren. Careful attention to the eminent historian's work must certainly have helped reinforce Bancroft's notions about history and have inspired him to emulation.

The first of Bancroft's translations from Heeren appeared in 1824 as *Reflections on the Politics of Ancient Greece*, which was sufficiently successful for a second edition to be called for in 1842 after its adoption as a textbook by Harvard.[29] In his translator's preface, Bancroft claims only the humble utility of "increasing the number of good books" available to Americans and thus aiding "the advancement of learning in our common country" (v, vi). But his grounds for recommending the work indicate that he already held that the historian was bound to seek general laws, "to study human nature, as exhibited in its grandest features in the change of nations" (vi). The common reader may thereby reach wiser decisions concerning the politics of his own times. Indicating his own leanings, Bancroft especially recommends Heeren's discussion of Demosthenes as refuting "the calumnies that have so long been heaped upon one of the noblest, most persevering, most disinterested advocates of the cause of suffering liberty" (vi).

Heeren's text contains a number of doctrines later echoed in Bancroft's *History*. While admitting, and even insisting, on the great varieties of constitutions found in Ancient Greece, Heeren found them all "free constitutions" (157), in which the norm was that "all magistrates must be appointed by the people" (172), and whose "chief object was the preservation of freedom and equality among the commons" (177). Admitting the instability of the constitutions, Heeren held that "in these, to all appearances, imperfect constitutions, everything, which forms the glory of man, flourished in its highest perfection" (179). He attributes the greatness of Greek art to its public character, and the decline of Greek civilization to moral decay.

Of equal or greater importance was Bancroft's translation (with some help) in 1828 of Heeren's *History of the Political System of Europe and its Colonies, from the Discovery of America to the Independence of the Continent*. This work covers ground that Bancroft later made his own, and he and his readers must have found congenial Heeren's friendly attitude toward the United States. Bancroft's 1854 oration on progress was to echo Heeren's vision of a universal, unified world order, a future "more glorious" because "more free."[30] To the translation Bancroft added extracts from a Heeren preface to a later edition in which Heeren wrote that man should be considered "an instrument of Providence, for purposes other and higher than his own" and that he had aimed to discuss events "according to political principles, which he regards as immutable" (I, viii). Bancroft refers to Heeren's work in several footnotes to the early volumes of the *History*.

Another Heeren translation was published earlier in 1828 at Northampton by the same publishers. Although it is not usually attributed to Bancroft, he wrote the preface, and no other name is given as concerned with translation. Probably he supervised the work, as he did with part of the *Political Systems*; he seems to refer to himself in the preface as "the editor."[31] The work is referred to in letters from Bancroft to President Kirkland that spring; and the second of these letters gives the first indication that Bancroft was thinking of writing history himself: the work would be a first step in "a complete course of History. The labor will be great. The History of the Middle [Ages?] I shall write myself, or perhaps abridge from some very useful books I have on that subject. For Modern Europe there is an excellent manual of Heeren. For our own country I should venture to write [some] lines."[3][2] The Heeren manual referred to was the *Political Systems*; Bancroft's work on his own country became not "some lines" but the ten volumes of the *History*.

But in one important respect Bancroft's *History* did not follow the lines of Heeren's manual. The *History of the States of Antiquity* is a dull, although well-organized, compendium of facts. It prefaces each period with an "account of the original sources, from which all knowledge of it must be derived" (iv) and with annotated references to modern works dealing with the period. Bancroft was in sympathy with Heeren's insistence on the critical use of sources and with his assumption that "Philosophical history ... flourishes best under free constitutions" (9); but Heeren's work is a barely readable reference manual, and Bancroft's preface to it indicates his own preference for historical writing "which combines eloquence of manner with the philosophical arrangement of facts" (iii). He had, after all, been steeping himself in German literature as well as in German historians. His apprenticeship over, he soon combined the romantic idealism of the poet with the careful research of the historians; the result would move men's hearts and make him famous.

IV   *Ideas in History*

As we turn to the first volume of the *History*, we may well ask what the "philosophical arrangement of facts" would mean for a young historian already committed to a belief in the inevitability of progress and self-government. Certainly it does not mean that philosophical ideas play a leading role in his story, even when he deals with the Puritans, an unusually intellectual and ideologically committed group.[3][3] Bancroft is not even especially apt at identifying ideas as causes of actions; the abstract ideas of Progress and Providence remain in the realm of final cause, of teleology, while the immediate causes assigned to events are the particular motives of the men and groups involved.

Bancroft's ideas did serve him as important guides to the selection and interpretation of his data, and it is in this sense that we may credit his *History* with a "philosophical arrangement of facts." Historical "facts" are in any case a slippery form of knowledge, since they are mere inferences from the actual historical remains of paper and stone, although historians of differing ideological persuasions may be able to agree on certain "facts." Moreover, most histories contain fewer "facts" than the historian has discovered; they are simply not part of the story he has chosen to tell. His choice of story is not a self-evident decision; he is guided by "certain dominant concepts or leading ideas," which seem to connect his facts.[34] In Bancroft's *History,* the ideas of progress and self-government which characterize his philosophy of history serve to provide a "narrative frame of reference," determining what story he has to tell.[35]

A historian may, like Leopold von Ranke, cherish the very "pastness' of the past; he may then wish to stress the characteristics of an era which mark it as unique. He may, like Edward Gibbon, aim to explain the loss of a Golden Age. For Bancroft, history was the progressive unfolding of the divine will; the significant events in the past were those which pointed to the future, and his object was to construct a narrative action leading toward the present. Bancroft's belief in progress thus led to a kind of "presentism" not uncommon among historians. Since he also saw the historian as a moral prophet, he was even more willing than most "presentist" historians to pass moral judgment upon the past.

Later historians have sometimes objected to the freedom with which Bancroft's belief in progress and moral judgments of historical events and characters finds expression in the *History*. But the notion that passing moral judgment is "unhistorical" is surely wrong. For some, this view rests on the assumption that historical narrative inevitably implies a causal chain, and that this determinsm is incompatible with passing moral judgment. But even if we admit that history may require a deterministic causality, it is simply naive to argue that determinism is incompatible with moral judgment.[36] We may say that to understand all is to forgive all; but, in understanding what leads a man to murder, we do not necessarily surrender the right to say that murder is a wrong act.

For some, the objection to Bancroft's moral judgments is really an objection to his presentism—to pass judgment on a man in 1634 on the basis of the moral standards of 1834 may be seen as a violation of the effort to enter sypathetically into the experience of the past. But even if we refuse to allow Bancroft his own conception of his role, this objection reduces itself to the assertion that we cannot understand a murderer without agreeing that his act was justified. Otherwise, we are left with only a moral demand that the historian enter into the values of a past he may understand without doing so.

The demand that he judge the past by its own values is, moreover, an impossible one, as moral demands so often are; for the individuals he deals with themselves hold differing values. For example, the Puritan's values differed in part from those of Roger Williams and from the English Church they resisted, and they differed a good deal from those of the Indians. To construct a history, the historian must show sympathetic understanding of all these groups, but it does him no good to simply surrender his own values for theirs. If he chooses to express his own value judgments, it does not necessarily follow that he is incapable of comprehending theirs.

The historian's predispositions may, of course, sometimes stand in the way of his understanding the past—Bancroft, for example, shows none of Parkman's ability to empathize with the Indians. But this will happen whether or not he chooses to express his values in his narrative. The argument that he should refrain from expressing his values fails to distinguish between the process by which the historian arrives at his image of the past and the manner in which he chooses to present it. We may hold that excessive authorial comment is a literary flaw, but knowing a historian's predispositions can help us make allowance for them.[37]

Bancroft's predispositions are clearly stated. He had been taught that the history of a people could be explained by reference to its spirit; and, as we have seen, he found in the American will to self-government an explanation for much of its history. This belief obviously influenced the selection and interpretation of materials for the first volume. His first task was to discuss in an organized manner the discovery of America and the founding of the first colonies. Because he thought the past relevant insofar as it helped to create the present, he chose to concentrate on the English colonies and, among these, the Puritan colonies, "for they are the parents of one-third the whole white population of the United States" (467-68).

The issues of civil polity dominate Bancroft's treatment of the first two Southern colonies, Maryland and Virginia. The early struggles of the Virginia colony are told in some detail, but the climax of Chapter IV, "The Colonization of Virginia," is the establishment of a colonial constitution, which is regarded by Bancroft as having freed the colonists from the control of Parliament while maintaining allegiance to the crown. It made the colony "a nursery of freemen," and it connected "popular freedom so intimately with the life, prosperity, and state of society in Virginia, that they could never be separated" (I, 158). What follows in the narrative concentrates on the colony's efforts to retain freedom from parliamentary authority and to limit the powers of the appointed governor: "Virginia had herself, almost unconsciously, established a nearly independent democracy; and already preferred her own sons for places of authority" (I, 232). Bancroft's account of the founding of Maryland in Chapter VI also ends by striking this note: "Thus was Maryland, like Virginia, at the epoch of the restoration, in full possession of liberty, based upon the practical assertion of the sovereignty of the people. Like Virginia, it had so nearly completed its institutions, that, till the epoch of its final separation from England, it hardly made any further advances towards freedom" (I, 265).

Bancroft deals with the New England colonies at greater length and with greater complexity but to the same end. The Puritans "planted in their hearts the undying principles of democratic liberty," and the volume ends with the question of whether the Restoration would allow the New Englanders, like their Southern compatriots, to retain "the benefits of self-government" (I, 469). Religious issues demand and secure treatment, but Bancroft is consistently more alive to their political than to their theological dimensions. His accounts of such conflicts as that over Roger Williams depend on the two senses in which a phrase like "democratic liberty" may be taken. Williams is seen as standing for "liberty" as an absolute; and Bancroft, like many of Williams's orthodox opponents, greatly admires him. But, in opposing the general will of the Massachusetts colony and in threatening its relations with England, Williams threatened the growth of "self-government." Bancroft concedes that the Puritans were intolerant, but he explains their intolerance by reference to their political situation rather than to their theological beliefs.[38]

If we conceive the historian as re-creating the past in its own terms, we might object that Bancroft fails to give religious issues their full weight. But Bancroft is operating within his own assumptions about the task of the historian; for him, the important elements in the past are those which look forward to what he deems the significant events of the future—the Revolution and the creation of the new republic. The same criterion guides his treatment of the internal struggles of the Bay Colony; and Bancroft is, of course, on the side of a more democratic government; more significantly, he regards the pressure from below for expansion of the power of the commons as the historically important fact. Some historians have identified the Puritans with clerical leaders like John Cotton or magistrates like John Winthrop, but the inevitable result of identifying the movement with its leaders is to see "Puritanism" as essentially anti-democratic, whether theocratic or oligarchic. For men like Cotton and Winthrop distrusted anything that smacked of pure democracy, and they sometimes resisted the rule of the people as vigorously as that of the King. For Bancroft, what counts is the evident feeling of the people as a whole, or of the freemen among them; from basically the same historical facts he can argue, therefore, that the two objects dearest to the emigrants were "Purity of religion and civil liberty" (I, 359).[39]

Given Bancroft's theory of progress, it is natural to see even faltering steps toward self-government as more important than occasional failures to match that ideal. Although Bancroft does not go much past the Stuart Restoration in this volume, occasional glances ahead show that he has no doubt of the reality of progress in history: "We admire the rapid growth of our cities; the sudden transformation of portions of the wilderness into blooming states. St. Augustine [Florida] presents a stronger contrast, in its transition from the bigoted policy of Philip II to the American principles of religious liberty. Its origin should be carefully remembered, for it is a fixed point, from which to measure the liberal influence of time; the progress of modern civilization; the victories of the American mind, in its contests for the interests of humanity" (I, 72). Because they contributed to this progress, Bancroft is willing to forgive the early Puritans much of what they did and stood for.

Progress is not only reality but a promise; and, to Bancroft, the promise is from God. History is guided by "The mysterious influence of that Power which enchains the destinies of states, overruling the decisions of sovereigns and the forethought of statesmen" (I, 266). In an aside, Bancroft assures his reader that the Puritan's intolerance is not needed to protect religion—"Atheism is a folly of the metaphysician, not the folly of human nature" (I, 447). Bancroft was not writing a theological tract, and such religious references are less common in his narrative than we might think if we read only historiographers' comments about his work. His belief in Providence and progress is important as one of the assumptions which helps him make the past intelligible. He was primarily telling a story; but he assumed, and most of his original readers were ready to assume with him, that the original Author was God and that some exalted destiny awaited America at the end of her part in the piece. This and other assumptions, obvious in the shaping of the first volume, are at work throughout the *History* as principles of selection and interpretation.

CHAPTER 2

Voting for Jackson

BANCROFT'S democratic bias in the first volume of his history was sufficiently obvious that many readers felt that it cast a ballot for Andrew Jackson. His Harvard friend George Ticknor remonstrated with him for seeking political advancement; and even Bancroft's brother-in-law, John Davis, the recently elected Whig governor of Massachusetts, thought it necessary to warn Bancroft on this point: "I would rather rest my reputation upon it with posterity than upon all the art of Jackson and Van [Buren] together, but let me entreat you not to let the partisan creep into the work. Do not imbue it with any present feeling or sentiment of the moment which may give impulse to your mind."[1] Bancroft's political leanings had been made obvious long enough before his writing the *History* to clear him of any charge of political opportunism. If his early path had made him see the historian as tracing the path to the present, the same influences had shaped his view of the politics of the present. However, Bancroft was perfectly aware that his work's democratic leanings had contemporary political implications. It earned him a number of enemies in Massachusetts; that it might earn him friends as well, he sent a copy of the first volume to Martin Van Buren, the master political strategist of the national Democratic party. A covering letter pointed out the attacks made on Bancroft by anti-democrats.

But most readers did not consider the *History* a political document; it would hardly have sold so widely or so well if they had done so. Many essentially conservative men admired Bancroft's achievement and said so, and one of these was his old Harvard friend, Edward Everett, now a prominent Whig and soon to review Bancroft's first volume in the *North American*. Everett wrote Bancroft a letter of praise for the book. "a Work which will last while the memory of America lasts; and which will instantly take its place among the classics of our language. It is full of learning, information, common sense and philosophy; full of taste and eloquence; full of life and power. . . . I could almost envy you to have found so noble a theme, while yet so young. You can bestow on it all the time it needs. Carry it on, and complete it before you reach the meridian."[2] Bancroft was not to complete his effort so quickly, for he was soon deeply involved in political affairs. In a few years he would play a major role in defeating an Everett bid for governor and do so in a way that brought a temporary break in their long friendship.

I   *The Scholar in Politics*

Bancroft's first public avowal of his political position occurred in 1826 when the town of Northampton asked him to deliver the annual Fourth of July oration. On this nonpartisan occasion, Bancroft's speech did not directly refer to current party politics; but it was not hard to see where he stood. His address identified the spirit of America with the principles of Thomas Jefferson. The people were to be supreme; the government must be a thorough-going democracy; and the voice of the people "is the voice of God."[3] These were not the sentiments of old New England, the conservative Boston Federalists who had never entirely trusted the Adamses of Quincy, the new Boston Whigs who stood for a government by élite and felt sure that they themselves constituted such an élite. Bancroft's father had been a conservative Federalist, his sister Eliza had recently married John Davis, and he himself was about to marry Sarah Dwight, whose family was as conservative as it was wealthy. Before the oration, he wrote a humorous warning to his fiancée: "If your father should think of coming, you must tell him what a radical, democratic, levelling, unrighteous oration I have written." Since Sarah herself was to be absent, Bancroft comforted himself with the thought that he would not wish her to be there unless he were certain of his being a success.[4]

The Whigs at this time controlled the political life of Massachusetts. Responsive to the dominant economic interests of the state, drawing their leaders from its social oligarchy, they were well entrenched. The Democratic opposition was small and weak, although Jackson's election had brought David Henshaw into the powerful patronage office of Collector of the Port of Boston. Moreover, the opposition was not even united since there were independent Anti-Masonic and Workingmen's parties competing for the anti-Whig vote. The problem was to unite these forces and find a popular issue. With the Democratic party controlling national politics, rewards were awaiting the man who could succeed in doing so.

Then as now, most American intellectuals were in general sympathy with movements for liberal reform, and Bancroft's own views may well have been affected by European liberal constitutionalists like Heeren. Then as now, many intellectuals disdained the necessities of practical politics; though Bancroft shared something of this disdain, he hungered for a large success in life and was willing to pay the price. His *History* would win the approval of the Whig elite, but Bancroft would not ally himself with them politically: "I remain firmly of the opinion," he wrote Everett, "that the man of letters must be the man of the people."[5] Personal resentments may also have played a part; Bancroft had never felt comfortable with the Boston aristocracy, and he had not enjoyed his time as an instructor at Harvard. His father had defied the clerical establishment in Massachusetts; Bancroft was about to defy its political establishment.

For a while after his marriage, Bancroft was relatively silent about political issues. Then, in 1830, he was nominated for state senator by the Workingmen's party. Bancroft refused the nomination, but the incident showed that he was a potential vote-getter and that his anti-Whig sympathies were at least suspected. Those who knew him best did not take his disclaimers of interest at full value: "Pray when did you bring those lurking desires after distinction under such severe discipline that they dare not jog your memory?" asked John Davis.[6] In January, 1831, Bancroft took a more positive step into the political arena by publishing an article in the *North American* about the Bank of the United States. Although Bancroft's original article contained no comment on the current bank controversy, and although the editors tacked on (without his knowledge) a paragraph favoring extension of the charter, the article as a whole clearly supported Jackson's attack on the bank and its privileges.

Bancroft's article created a small controversy of its own, not least within the Dwight family, which had banking interests. He wrote his wife in May: "Your Uncle Ned told at a dinner party, that the article on the Bank was written under your father's dictation, simply in defense of your father's interests. ... This Edmund said at his own table with Webster, Story, & others at it. Judge ye."[7] Bancroft soon lectured his wife's uncle "on his ignorance and folly about the matter; and gave him plainly to understand, he might read what I should write, to learn; and not undertake to criticize."[8] Bancroft was always very sensitive about slights upon his honor, but it is true that many of the smaller banks resented the powers of the Bank of the United States;

hearing that Bancroft was to write about the bank, another of her uncles, Henry Dwight of the Bank of Michigan, had advised him "that the best ground to take is that the Bank is not to be renewed at all."[9]

Although John Davis was sympathetic, Boston reaction in general was not. The *North American* would not allow Bancroft to reply to an answering article by Alexander Everett, who also saw fit to write Bancroft to warn him against connecting himself in any way with the Workingmen's party—"I look upon it as nothing more or less than Jacksonism disguised."[10] If the Whigs of Massachusetts did not appreciate Bancroft's article, he knew who would; and he made sure that a copy was given to Martin Van Buren. During the following year he was able to visit the capital himself, partly on Dwight family business, partly in order to see various politicians, purposes not always entirely separate. There he found that his views on the Bank question pleased administration figures, and he made sure that his views were made known to them. Curiously enough, he was not especially impressed by the President: "I am not among the admirers of General Jackson. He has not the marks of greatness about him."[11]

The controversy made Bancroft's name even more attractive to editors and booksellers, but most of his energies were going into his *History*. When he traveled for the Dwights, he contrived to search also for papers that might be of use to him. He believed himself that his new contacts were of use to him, too: "My former years you know passed rather among books and boys than in action. It has been a benefit to me to have mingled actively among men: I understand them better than before."[12] As oft happens with scholars, the more Bancroft read the more he became convinced that his predecessors had fallen down on the job: "I am surprised at the tissues of fables, which so wise a man as Chief Justice Marshall has been willing to endorse. Judge Story in his introductory chapters has committed some strange errors. He is wrong, though a judge."[13] Recognition of his predecessor's errors did not prevent him from soliciting Story's comments, among others, on the advance sheets of the first volume; from such comments he could sense its impending success, and even before the appearance in print of the first volume, he was at work on continuations.[14]

The success of the *History* naturally increased Bancroft's political attractiveness. The Whigs had already sensed Bancroft's talents and offered him the appointive post of secretary of state in Massachusetts. Bancroft would have made a good Whig: he was connected by marriage and friendship with prominent Whigs like Davis and Everett; he was well known as a writer for the prestigious journals; and he was popular in a rural area where the party was relatively weak. His refusal can be attributed either to his devotion to democracy or to his realization that the Democrats were bound to win in the long run. It certainly cannot be attributed to a lack of interest in politics, for he responded eagerly in 1834 when Henshaw finally asked him to attend the state Democratic convention. That same year he attended the state Anti-Masonic convention, where he seems to have tricked the party leaders into certifying that he had been nominated for Congress. He publicly turned down another offer from the Whigs, and he refused another nomination from the Workingmen's party. Having shown widespread appeal, he showed his party loyalty by campaigning vigorously for Marcus Morton, the Democratic candidate for governor in 1835 and 1836. In 1836, Bancroft formally became a member of the Democratic party.

Bancroft brought a number of advantages to the Democrats. The party needed a respectable scholar-orator to match Whigs like Webster and Everett. Bancroft's oratorical style had not won great favor in the pulpit, but it seemed right for Fourth of July orations. The various anti-Whig parties had no common program nor any basis for one save a common distrust of the Whigs, but Bancroft could clothe this feeling with words which elevated it to a philosophy of government, one practically co-extensive with the American way of life. Granting that the Whigs were patriotic Americans and not mere reactionary Tories, he grants them scarcely any other virtue:

The tory idolizes power; the whig worships his interests; democracy struggles for equal rights. The tory pleads for absolute monarchy; the whig for the wealthy aristocracy; democracy for the power of the people. The tory regards liberty as a boon; the whig regards it as a fortunate privilege; democracy claims freedom as an inalienable right. The tory loves to see a slave at the plough; the whig prefers a tenant or a mortgaged farm; democracy puts the plough in the hands of the owner. . . . The tory adheres to the party of Moloch; the whig still worships at the shrine of Mammon; democracy is practical Christianity.[15]

Some Mammon-worshipping Whigs were displeased by Bancroft's equation of democracy, even in the small case, with Christianity. One respectable Bostoner wrote of Bancroft as a traitor to his class: "Bancroft is abundantly supplied with property and has turned renegade to make himself of consequence in a line wholly unsuited to his character. It is a pity that he should have left the true path clearly marked out for him, as he could have done himself and his country most by keeping in it. The first volume of his history was exceedingly suitable, but his new pursuits will take away all confidence in his statements, as he has thus early notoriously falsified facts having a political cast."[16] But orations of this sort—and copies thoughtfully distributed to influential Democrats—helped Bancroft make a political reputation which brought him the Democratic nomination for Congress in 1836. He lost, as he must have expected to; but he was now firmly established as one of the state's leading Democrats. The party's fortunes, too, were sufficiently improved for the share to be worth having—in eight years the Democratic share of the gubernatorial vote had risen from twelve per cent to forty-six per cent.

Even while maneuvering to establish himself in the counsels of the Democratic party, Bancroft was working hard on his second volume, which was to confirm his reputation as a historian. He assured his correspondents that the task engaged him "day and night,"[17] and he often managed to write for fourteen or fifteen hours by rising at five to begin his day. The success of his first volume eased his way in searching out relevant documents, and friends and strangers wrote to call his attention to papers they had come across. When the new volume appeared in 1837, it repeated and enhanced the success of its predecessor. The young Transcendentalist editor Orestes Brownson called it "the best historical production in our language. What is more to the point, I say honestly, that in my opinion, it is destined to do more for the cause of our principles, universal liberty, than any other work in the English language."[18]

The success of the second volume was all that Bancroft had to rejoice about for most of 1837. Shortly before its appearance, and soon after the birth of a third child, Sarah Bancroft died. The children were placed in the care of one of Bancroft's sisters, and he was left alone with his work as a historian and with his ambitions as a politician. It was also a year of political disappointment for the economy had gone into a tailspin, which the Whigs were successful in blaming on the policies of the Democratic national administration. The result was a serious defeat for the Democrats in Massachusetts, despite their success in winning to their side the Anti-Masonic machine of Benjamin Hallett and most of the Workingmen's leaders. Morton's percentage of the gubernatorial vote declined for the first time.

The party's troubles were to be Bancroft's opportunity. The defeat and the campaign which had preceded it led to a final break between Morton and David Henshaw, who for years were the co-leaders of the Massachusetts Democrats. Despite Henshaw's control of patronage, Morton held the allegiance of the party rank-and-file and was closest to the new elements in the Democratic coalition. Most important of all, Morton proved to have the best connections in Washington and succeeded in having Henshaw replaced as Collector of the Port of Boston for 1838. Morton did not want the post for himself; various names were considered, but George Bancroft was chosen as one who had shown himself popular with the Anti-Masons and with Workingmen and as a non-Bostonian whose appointment might please rural voters. Urging him to accept, Morton promised to use his influence to secure Bancroft "any other situation, at home or abroad, which shall be more compatible with your pursuits and more congenial to your taste, whenever your services in this, shall have ceased to be necessary."[19]

Some of Bancroft's friends also thought the collectorship an incongruous post for the historian. William Prescott, for whose *Ferdinand and Isabella* Bancroft was busy securing good reviews from Democratic organs, sent sarcastic compliments about Bancroft's having received "the high and responsible and *literary* post of the Customs," trusting that this "lucrative" position would enable him to spend some time still in "the noblest, and certainly the most independent career offered to man."[20] Bancroft later felt that the collectorship "did not indemnify me for the cost of changing residence and loss of time,"[21] but its secure income of some five thousand dollars a year was not unwelcome at the time, even if it was unnecessary.

To Bancroft, not income but power was the great attraction of the collectorship. Besides patronage in the form of jobs, there were a great many printing contracts to bestow. With such contracts as a dependable source of income, Bancroft was able to start a newspaper, the *Bay State Democrat*, to serve as a vehicle for his views and those of the party. With jobs at his disposal, Bancroft consolidated his power within the Democratic party; but his two most notable appointments were those he gave to Nathaniel Hawthorne and Orestes Brownson, whose political independence later caused Bancroft and his party a certain amount of embarassment (Nye, 124). Bancroft's new political power was also used in securing Henry Dwight's Bank of Michigan an extension of time in repaying a debt to the United States government.[22]

Soon after moving to Boston, Bancroft became involved in a public controversy with J. G. Palfrey, the editor of the *North American*, over yet another series of unauthorized emendations of a Bancroft review. Bancroft's sensitivity to any questioning of his integrity had reached new highs. Although he moved easily among Boston intellectuals, some still regarded him with suspicion, the result of a feeling, still current, that the scholar who writes of power from outside must be naive and the one who writes from inside must be corrupt.

Bancroft's move to Boston was brightened by his new acquaintance-ship with Elizabeth Davis Bliss. She was the sister of John Davis, already Bancroft's brother-in-law by marriage to his sister Eliza. Elizabeth, a widow with two children, was to provide him with the stable home life he needed for his work. As she wrote a relative, she found him "ardent, enthusiastic, warm-hearted, and yet rigid and unbending in his convictions where a principle is involved. . . . Your Uncle Morton and I, as you well know, do not belong to the daring or fearless class, and I think a little mixture will be no injury to the 'blood' as he and Thomas call it."[23] The new Mrs. Bancroft was annoyed to find that some of her friends felt she had married a political adventurer; but, without expressing great interest in politics herself, she pledged to follow Bancroft wherever his destiny might lead him.[24]

The election of 1838 was another defeat for the Democrats but a less serious one than that of the year before. When Bancroft's old friend Edward Everett was elected governor, he soon handed Bancroft and the Democrats a winning issue by signing a bill making illegal the sale of liquor in less than fifteen gallon lots. The bill was not part of the Whig legislative program, but the Whig governor's signature on the bill confirmed for many a lower-class voter the impression that the Whigs cared only for the rich—those who could afford the legal measure of whiskey—and nothing for the poor, who could not. The campaign of 1839 centered on this issue, which had the great advantage of providing a focus for the disparate elements of the Democratic coalition; and, after years of trying, Morton was finally elected Governor. Bancroft could feel that his venture into politics had achieved some measure of success. In the same year Mrs. Bancroft brought forth a daughter and Bancroft himself a third volume of his *History*, completing the first unit—the history of the colonization. His friend Prescott returned past favors with a review in the *North American* giving Bancroft a "place among the great historical writers of the age" (Nye, 123). Successful for the moment in both of his chosen careers, Bancroft would not find it so easy in the future to combine them.

At first, it seemed as if his political career would be short-lived. In

1840 Van Buren was at the head of the ticket; and four years of economic difficulty and political controversy made the incumbent President a liability to his party—all the more so because of the contrast between his urbane manners and the rustic ways of the Whig candidate, William Henry Harrison. This contrast made the election especially difficult for a Democratic machine like that in Massachusetts, which was built around the common man's enmity toward the Boston Establishment. The gubernatorial campaign might in any case have been lost; for, since the Whig candidate was the familiar John Davis rather than the unfortunate Everett, the liquor-law issue could play no part. Bancroft allowed his paper to accuse his brother-in-law of grafting, but to no avail. Morton's loss was in many ways less serious than Van Buren's in its effects on the Massachusetts party, for loss of the Presidency meant the loss of the Federal patronage on which the party had come to depend to maintain and discipline its organization. As collector, Bancroft was, of course, one of the first to go.

The loss of the collectorship gave Bancroft more time to work on the continuation of his *History*, but the work went slowly. With the history of the colonization behind him, Bancroft planned to deal with the period from 1748 to 1789 in another three or four volumes; in April, 1844, he hoped to have the first of those volumes published and in three or four years to have completed the whole.[25] It was to take him much longer, both in time and number of volumes. "Is not the American Revolution a subject worth delaying upon?" he asked in self-defense, adding that the very mass of new material he was uncovering made it more difficult for him to organize his work.[26] He prepared an abridgment of the first three volumes, aiming it at the school market; but its sales were far below expectations; and the publishers, Little and Brown, blamed this fact on the high copyright price demanded by Bancroft.[27] Occasional journal contributions and public lectures also helped keep Bancroft's name before the public; everywhere he lectured, he sought out relevant historical documents. He seems to have written a long narrative poem in this period, but he did not publish it.[28]

But Bancroft had not chosen to retire into the life of a scholar. His lecture tours served also to maintain and widen his national political contacts. In the meantime, President Harrison's death and John Tyler's succession had rendered his position in Massachusetts itself precarious. Tyler and John Calhoun, out to mould a new kind of party, provided a comeback for the ousted David Henshaw. Benjamin Hallett, having led his forces from Anti-Masonry into the Morton-Bancroft wing of the Democratic party, now appeared ready to join Henshaw and Rantoul, the Tyler-appointed collector. Morton won the governorship by a political accident in 1842 but lost it again in 1843. If the Tyler-Calhoun faction could win the Presidency in 1844, Morton and Bancroft could hardly expect to retain much power among the Massachusetts Democrats. But, since Bancroft and his friends still retained the loyalty of most of the rural Democrats, they managed to control the Massachusetts delegation to the 1844 national convention. Bancroft went to it pledged to Van Buren, but he proved more flexible than loyal when a deadlock developed between Van Buren and Lewis Cass of Michigan. He played a prominent role in the negotiations that led to the nomination of James K. Polk.

Bancroft was forced to run for office himself that fall, for Morton had grown tired of his annual and usually unsuccessful race for the governor's chair. An unfamiliar name at the head of the ticket, Bancroft lost badly. The campaign brought more personal attacks on Bancroft by his old enemies among the Boston Whigs, while many of his friends among Boston intellectuals were alienated by his advocating the annexation of Texas. Increasingly interested in politics, Mrs. Bancroft admired her husband's bravery in facing so much vilification; but Bancroft professed himself unbothered—"And if I have a woman that loves me, what care I for a party that strives to annoy me?"[29] He campaigned out of the state as well as in Massachusetts, but he managed to spend a good part of his time working on his history.

Bancroft had no strong interest in serving as governor and no desire to return to the collectorship, but he did covet a diplomatic appointment and felt that his role in securing President Polk's nomination had earned him the right to expect one. Instead, he was named Secretary of the Navy and given the promise of a future appointment abroad. Even this appointment did not go unchallenged; his enemies in the Massachusetts Democratic party charged that Bancroft was an Abolitionist, and his confirmation was delayed in the Senate. But when Polk stood firm and when the charge could not be proved, Bancroft was eventually confirmed. Before leaving Boston, he took a hand in parceling out patronage, not controlled by Morton as the new collector; Bancroft reportedly took special pleasure in leaving unsatisfied the unreliable Hallett.

Bancroft found his new post, relatively unbothered by patronage seekers, "altogether the pleasantest in the government," and he claimed to regard the Secretary of the Treasury with compassion.[30] His service as Secretary of the Navy was relatively short but relatively distinguished: he curtailed the use of flogging as a punishment; he improved the operations of the Naval Observatory; and he established the Naval Academy at Annapolis. Although proposals for such an academy had been made before, they had always failed to win Congressional approval; and Bancroft was not too immodest in asserting (in a private letter) that it "was my original conception, mine alone, and in every particular carried out by me."[31] By clever use of his powers as Secretary and by careful budgeting, Bancroft was able to establish the Academy as a going operation even before asking Congress for annual funding.

Bancroft's most serious responsibilities as Secretary came after May 31, 1845, when he found himself made Acting Secretary of War. It was Bancroft who ordered Zachary Taylor to the banks of the Rio Grande; who sent John Frémont on a "scouting" expedition to California; who wrote standing instructions ordering an American fleet to proceed to California if war should break out. The policy was President Polk's, for he wished to obtain California by negotiation or by force. Inside the cabinet, Bancroft opposed Polk's desire to declare war even before the skirmish at the Rio Grande offered a handy pretext; still, when the time came, Bancroft helped Polk draft his message to Congress. Bancroft also did his best to placate his New England friends who feared that the annexation of Texas and war with Mexico could only advance the interests of the "slave power." The conflict, as divisive as the war in Vietnam in our own era, further alienated Bancroft from some of his friends in the American intellectual community.

Although Bancroft worked hard and effectively at his cabinet post, he did not forget his desire to serve abroad, and he did not allow Polk to forget it. At last, when he was offered his choice of service in London or Paris, he chose London and sailed for his new position in October, 1846. It was seven years since the third volume of his *History* had appeared; it would be nearly six more years before the next two of his volumes would be published. Bancroft's political career had brought him to a level of service which did not allow him to devote full time to his History. But it had also brought him knowledge of the living flow of history; and, in his new appointment, he had an ideal opportunity to obtain access to foreign archives. The appointment delayed the appearance of his *History* but enriched its content.

II *Democracy and Democrats*

Most of the *History* was written while Bancroft was actively engaged in partisan politics; the question inevitably arises to what degree his party activities were reflected in his historical writing. It is possible to conceive of an entire history constructed on partisan principles and designed to justify by an appeal to past history the present political positions of a political party or faction. Bancroft's history clearly does not fall in this category. On the other hand, we may feel sure that a historian's understanding of past political processes is partly shaped by his present experience. This truism no doubt applies to Bancroft, though we can hardly prove it, but it is too general to help us in the analysis of Bancroft's treatment of political topics. The question before us, then, lies between these two poles: whether Bancroft's contemporary political commitments can be shown to have significantly shaped his interpretation of specific events in the past.

Although his first preface spoke of carrying forward his *History* "to the present time" (I, v), Bancroft called a temporary halt to his work in his Notice in Volume III:

This volume completes the History of the Colonization of the United States. In the arrangement of my subject, the great drama of their Independence opens with the attempts of France and England to carry the peace of Aix into effect. Should the propriety of the time selected for the division be questioned, I will ask, for the present, a suspension of judgment.

If my labors thus far are accepted by my country, no higher reward can be hoped for, than to hear, from the favoring opinion of the people, the summons to go forward, and write the History of the American Revolution, achieved by our fathers, not for themselves and their posterity only, but for the world. (III, ix)

This statement really signifies no more than that Bancroft had completed the first unit of the *History*. The request for suspended judgment shows that he had already received sufficient assurance of the people's favor in the reviews of his two earlier volumes and in his royalty receipts. The next three volumes of his history, published after his return from Great Britain, were also conceived as a unit. The Preface to Volume VI explains that "The present Volume completes the History of the American Revolution, considered in its causes. The last three explain the rise of the union of the United States from the body of the people, the change in the colonial policy of France, and the consequences of the persevering ambition of Great Britain to consolidate its power over America. The penal acts of 1774 dissolved the moral connection between the two countries, and began the civil war" (VI, iii). The rationales given for the two units illustrate the two ways in which Bancroft views colonial history: as part of a rational power struggle between European powers and as a providential growth to moral independence on the part of the colonies. The "union" of the colonies arises "from the body of the people"; and these volumes, like the earlier ones, reflect Bancroft's democratic bias. This bias, however, is probably best thought of as a philosophic predisposition reflected in both his work and his politics, stemming from neither.

Volume II, while carrying forward the stories of the colonies whose founding was recorded in Volume I, tells of the colonization of the Carolinas, the New Netherlands, and Pennsylvania. Bancroft is especially sympathetic to the Quakers and to William Penn, "the venerable apostle of Equality" (II, 402); and the relative freedom and prosperity of the Quaker colony is contrasted with the rule of royal governors in New York. A closing chapter, "The Result So Far," summarizes the result of a story traced "almost exclusively from contemporary documents and records" (II, 450) and provides a convenient summation of Bancroft's attitudes. The colonization of America is compared to the introduction of Christianity into Rome: it "was the most momentous event of the seventeenth century. The elements of our country, such as she exists today, were already there" (II, 451). The historian thus may seek in the past the outlines of the present.

Bancroft then pauses to review for several pages the religious history of Western Europe, finding the seeds of freedom in the Reformation, which "was the common people awakening to freedom of mind" (II, 454). Putting his point pithily for a change, Bancroft says: "Election implies faith, and faith freedom" (II, 463). What is important is not the doctrinal differences between the Antinomians and the Quakers, but their common allegiance to freedom of conscience. And this doctrine, indeed, appears more important than its religious garb—"The principle of freedom of mind, first asserted for the common people, under a religious form" (II, 463). Bancroft's training in divinity had not left him ignorant of the theological controversies of the past; but, since he was writing a basically political history his focus is on the political implications of religious statements. "The period through which we have passed shows why we are a free people; the coming period will show why we are a united people" (II, 466).

Bancroft's third volume carries the story of the colonies forward to the mid-eighteenth century. Much of the narrative is devoted to the background of the coming struggle between the great powers; one full chapter is devoted to the culture of the Indians. Once again, the close of his volume inspires Bancroft to make some general reflections on his task: "The moral world is swayed by general laws" (III, 397). "By comparison of document with document; by an analysis of facts, and the reference of each of them to the laws of the human mind which it illustrates; by separating the idea which inspires combined action from the forms it assumes; by comparing events with the great movement of humanity,—historic truth may establish itself as a science; and the principles that govern human affairs, extending like a path of light from century to century, become the highest demonstration of the superintending providence of God" (III, 398). The providential theory of history thus resembles laissez-faire economics: out of the selfish policies of greedy colonial powers the invisible hand of God created American independence. The process is like that of the Creation: "The political world was without form and void; yet the spirit of God was moving over the chaos of human passions and human caprices, bringing forth the firm foundations on which better hopes were to rest" (III, 400). In an era in which America's attention was turning inward, Bancroft's intense patriotism may have had as much to do with his popular appeal as did his championship of the common man.

In the three volumes which carry the story forward to 1748, Bancroft's philosophical asides grow less frequent; but his ardent patriotism remains. As before, each movement toward liberty is made by the people as a whole; the narrative is full of personified polities—"Massachusetts spoke through its House of Representatives" (V, 378). But this, too, is as much indicative of a romantic nationalism as it is of democratic sentiments. Still less can the democratic sentiments found in these volumes be properly ascribed to Bancroft's Jacksonian politics alone. Volumes II through VI simply show that the principles stated in his first volume and found earlier in his 1826 Fourth of July address remained a part of his intellectual furnishings. A slightly more understanding view of Great Britain appears in volumes IV through VI; it may reflect his residence in that country, but it could equally well be attributed to his use of its archives which would inevitably help him appreciate the motives of its statesmen. Suspicion of Great Britain was one of the attitudes which distinguished Democrats from their political opponents, but it was hardly a party stand.

One possible sign of Bancroft's devotion to the party of Jackson is the presence of occasional remarks which seem to anticipate Frederick Jackson Turner's belief that the frontier experience helped shape America. Certainly Bancroft believed that there was much that was unique about the American environment and experience: "Nothing came from Europe but a free people. . . . Like Moses, they had escaped from Egyptian bondage to the wilderness" (II, 451-52); yet this statement more closely echoes the Puritan image of themselves as the new children of Israel. Part of Bancroft's general romanticism, his love of freedom appears as a natural phenomenon once the social system of Europe has been escaped: "Overwhelmed in Europe, popular liberty, like the fabled fountain of the sacred Arethusa, gushed forth profusely in remoter fields" (II, 452). In this natural state, the Indians had a government "conducted harmoniously by the influence of native genius, virtue, and experience" (III, 275); by implication (II, 452), this is a polity much like that which sprang up naturally among their superior white successors in Virginia. His portrait of Daniel Boone (VI, 298-306) is a romantic picture of the frontiersman as one who "communed familiarly with the whole universe of life. Nature was his intimate" (VI, 301).[32]

But if Bancroft had been enough of an outsider early in life to have sympathy with mankind's outcasts, he had become enough of an insider to distrust certain popular movements. He praises Nathaniel Bacon, but he has no great respect for his followers in the Virginia rebellion of 1676: "An uneducated people obeys promptly the first call to action for freedom; it is less capable of union and perseverance" (II, 229). Bancroft admires the bravery of the North Carolina Regulators and sympathizes openly with their grievances, but he refers to them as "ignorant, though well-meaning husbandmen" (VI, 185). He liked revolutions best when they had a Washington at their head. In any case, anyone wishing to argue that Bancroft's love of frontier liberty was conditioned by his eventual admiration of General Jackson should remember that Bancroft first came to political power as a Massachusetts ally of the urbane Martin Van Buren.

If there is only this ambiguous evidence for the influence of the Jackson frontier image on Bancroft, there is even less evidence in the early volumes of the *History* of the great issue of the Bank, which launched Bancroft's career as a Jacksonian. Economic matters are in any case less important in Bancroft than they would be in a more modern account. He shows no special animus against British economic interests, even the East India Company, although he condemns the British government's mercantile policy designed to advance those very interests. Economic issues, like religious issues, are transformed into political issues. Bancroft seems in any case to have been one of those Jacksonians who opposed the Bank less because it was an economic monopoly than because it seemed linked with the principle of aristocracy. It is true that his political opponents in Massachusetts were members of an aristocratic elite, but Bancroft had never until the *History* been rich enough to be a full member of that group. Like the English aristocracy it aped, it was open to those who rose through merit, and it helped Bancroft on his rise; but his arrogance of manner reflected a real sensitivity to slights real and imagined. The roots of his opposition to aristocracy are not clear, but they lie deeper than his partisan allegiance.

So it is with most of the elements in the *History* which might be thought of as Jacksonian in temper: Bancroft's views were those formed long before his formal entry into party politics. His principles, after all, were shared by a preponderance of Bay State intellectuals; although few of them were partisan Democrats, George Ripley could fairly say that "Almost to a man, those who show any marks of genius or intellectual enterprise are philosophical democrats" (Nye, 119). Those who did not care to mingle with the sweaty crowd in politics, those who preferred the respectability of the high-minded Whigs—these might still find a hope in one of the many reform movements of the era. The Whigs' nomination of General Harrison in 1840 may have been political opportunism, but it indicated the spirit of the times; Bancroft's democratic views were thus readily acceptable to both the inner circle of critics and to the general public, regardless of party. His patriotism?—Well, no man has ever done poorly by telling a nation that it is great, if he be eloquent enough; and Bancroft was both eloquent and sincere.

III   *Free Men and Slaves*

George Bancroft's first Fourth of July oration was given in 1820 when he was a student at Göttingen. The only other American there at the time was a Professor Patton from Middlebury College in Vermont; and the two homesick Americans arranged a two-man banquet with poetry, orations, and toasts. The seventh of the twelve toasts was to "The Speedy Abolition of Slavery. May our country learn to practice at home the sublime lesson she has taught the world" (Howe, I, 76).

The toast, whether Bancroft's or Patton's, represents an anti-slavery stand which Bancroft held to throughout his life.

Slavery was the great moral issue of the years in which the first volumes of the *History* were published; it was also an issue which threatened to tear apart the party with which Bancroft had identified himself politically. The Democratic party was the one truly national political party, and it did its best to obscure, ignore, and patch up the fundamental differences within the party over slavery. The price of power within the party was discretion in expressing anti-slavery views, and Bancroft was willing to pay it. In 1834, before he became a Democrat, he gave in Northampton an oration entitled "The Influence of Slavery upon the Political Revolutions in Rome" which blamed slavery for the decline of Rome; but this statement was to be his last public utterance on the issue for many years. While it seems unlikely that Bancroft was temperamentally inclined to be a radical Abolitionist, it seems clear that he abhorred the institution of slavery; it seems equally that his long public silence on the issue was dictated partly by political considerations. Although his enemies had tried to hold up his appointment to the cabinet by claiming he was an Abolitionist, he had said nothing in his 1844 campaign for governor to appeal to the ten thousand voters who supported the Abolitionist candidate. The inevitable question is whether the *History* reflects his known views or his political ambitions, and the answer is that it places him squarely among the anti-slavery forces.

Bancroft's most lengthy discussion of the topic appears in the first volume; and it may be significant that this volume was published before Bancroft was formally allied with the Massachusetts Democrats. Slavery, which is accorded most of a chapter, is from the first stigmatized by Bancroft as unnatural in a free society; he endeavors to place the blame on the (primarily British) traders who brought the slave to America rather than on the planters who bought him: "While Virginia, by the concession of a representative government, was constituted the asylum of liberty, by one of the strange contradictions in human affairs, it became the abode of hereditary bondsmen. The unjust, wasteful and unhappy system was fastened upon the rising institutions of America, not by consent of the corporation, nor the desires of the emigrants; but, as it was introduced by the mercantile avarice of a foreign nation, so it was subsequently riveted by the policy of England, without regard to the interests or the wishes of the colony"

(I, 159). We note that the argument is not economic—that the bulk of the emigrants would have preferred not to compete with slave labor—but political—that the people, without outside interference, would have preferred free institutions.

Not content to clear the United States of the onus of having sought out the evil, Bancroft also maintains that "The spirit of the Christian religion would, before the discovery of America, have led to the entire abolition of the slave-trade, but for the hostility between the Christian churches and the followers of Mahomet" (I, 163), who enslaved captured Christians and so legitimated similar treatment of captured Moslems. Even so, by "the discovery of America, the moral opinion of the world had abolished the traffic in Christian slaves" (I, 165). But the practice of enslaving Negroes and Indians was well established even before the colonization of America; the first colonists simply took over the practice of those who had gone before.

America's long acceptance of slavery is obviously an uncomfortable point for Bancroft, as it would be for anyone with so exalted an opinion of the common man. Bancroft is too honest to conceal from the reader that even the most honorable of early settlers acquiesced in the practice—"The excellent Winthrop enumerates Indians among his bequests" (I, 168). He can only conclude that for once "The universal public mind was long and deeply vitiated" (I, 169). He lays repeated stress on its unchristian character; for once, the anti-clerical Bancroft does not scruple to quote the Pope—in fact, several Popes. The pleas of George Fox and Roger Williams for fixed terms of servitude are noted. The Dutch are blamed for the initial trade, "but the traffic would have been checked in its infancy, had its profits remained with the Dutch" (I, 177). The planters also profited and were blinded by their profits; and worst of all were the English slave traders. Even so, Bancroft makes the point that the slave population of the South was not large at the time of the Revolution.

Bancroft solves part of his ideological problem by noting that slavery in the South was supported by landed aristocrats after it had been introduced by foreign traders. He observes that Virginia law was less tolerant of slaves than many an earlier society, for slaves had in fact no human rights at all. His analysis remains political: "The institution of slavery," in turn, "renewed a landed aristocracy, closely resembling the feudal nobility" (II, 194). Virginia became torn between "a people" and "a rising aristocracy" (II, 195), but the balance was shifted by the restoration of the English monarchy, which favored the aristocracy.

The early history of the Northern states also speaks of slavery. Bancroft knows "That New York is not a slave-state like Carolina, is due to climate, and not to the superior humanity of its founders" (II, 303), although he refers not so much to the emigrants as to the colonial power, "the city of Amsterdam" (II, 303). The Quakers "agreed with the red man to love one another" (II, 401) but at first failed to do as much for the black man. But, if William Penn died a slaveholder, those Quakers who came from Germany believed in equality of all races before God. For Bancroft, the establishment of slavery in American can only be expiated by carrying out the pious promises of some of its earliest promoters, by giving to the Negro the blessings of Christianity and civilization so that he might, "in the end, be benefitted by the crimes of mercantile avarice" (II, 465).

In the third volume, Bancroft returns to the theme of British insistence on slavery in the colonies: "The party of the slave trade dictated laws to England" (III, 412). Bancroft notes that even the Southern colonies on occasion expressed opposition to the slave trade, but he also notes that "the question of abolishing slavery rested on different grounds. The one related to a refusal of trust; the other, to the manner of its exercise" (III, 410). If the Negro had been white, he would not have remained enslaved—"In the skin lay unexpiated, and, as it was held, inexpiable guilt" (III, 410). Because of the slave's physical constitution, slavery became "essentially a southern institution: to the southern colonies, mainly, Providence entrusted the guardianship and the education of the colored race" (III, 408). Bancroft does not hold back the failure of Christians to act on their principles, but he returns again to the issue of the slave trade and "its gigantic character of crime" (III, 412). Anxious to monopolize the slave trade with America, England forced the founders of Georgia to sanction slavery there and would not allow the colonists to restrict the trade in any way. But was it not the people of the colonies who provided the customers for the trade? Bancroft does not deny it, but he phrases it in a way unusual in one so often concerned to stress the Americanness of the colonies: "The Englishman in America tolerated and enforced" slavery on the black man.

The three volumes about the history of the colonization provide, in effect, the social background for the rest of the drama. In what follows, Bancroft is more frequently following a narrative line, and we find fewer references to slavery. Such references as there are are unfavorable: In New England, "Of slavery there was not enough to affect the character of the people" (IV, 150). The slave trade is still blamed on the British (V, 413-15). In his later accounts of the battles of the Revolution, he praises black troops (VIII, 232-33; X, 133). A long chapter in Volume X (1874), "The Rise of Free Commonwealths" (X, 345-70), deals with slavery at some length.

In any event, we find no evidence that Bancroft has played down his views on slavery or softened his expression of them for political reasons. The harshest comments on slavery come in the earliest volumes, published when Bancroft was just fashioning a political career for himself and when anti-slavery sentiment was far less common in the North than later; for his aversion to slavery was early formed and long retained. His treatment of the subject is unusual in some respects, but he was not attempting to extenuate the practice of his Southern brethren in the Democratic party. He was trying instead to fit the existence of slavery into his scheme of history, and his shifts and evasions result from the difficulty of reconciling the peculiar institution with the equality and dignity of man, with the moral progress of the race, and with the divine mission of the United States.

CHAPTER 3

Narrative Synthesis

WHEN we say that Bancroft was a great narrative historian, much depends on what we mean by a "historical narrative." One customary distinction is between the "chronicle" and the "narrative." In both cases the Aristotelian "object of imitation" cannot be the past itself but the historian's "imagined picture of the actual event."[1] The "chronicle," however, presents us with a more or less arbitrary selection of past events; in the "narrative" the historian has succeeded in comprehending the events with which he deals as part of a single "story." We have already seen that Bancroft's philosophic and political commitments provided him with a "narrative frame of reference" within which he could place the events of American history. To speak of his achievement as a narrative historian, then, is to evaluate his success in fitting the known events of the past into a kind of "synthetic unity" not found in mere chronicles.[2]

The processes of inference and deduction whereby a historian arrives at his historical "facts" are of interest chiefly to historiographers, though if he is proved inaccurate his history has failed on all counts. But a narrative synthesis of those facts is a literary, as well as historiographical, achievement. Bancroft's *History* is good literature as well as good history, not because of his style, which sometimes offends modern tastes, but because of his success in imposing form on his materials.[3] Having already considered the ideas which governed his choice of form, we must now consider its arrangement, under the general headings of scene, plot, and character.

I   *"Scene" in Bancroft's Narrative*

The unity of a historical narrative may derive from various sources—themes, social structures, or (in biographies) principal agents—but in Bancroft's *History* the unity is provided by a "plot," a series of lines of action interacting with each other.[4] Nevertheless, the volumes include many details which have no immediate connection with the principal lines of action in the work. Not part of the formal unity of the work, such details are part of its "representation," providing a scene for the action.

Some such "scenic" details serve to give a sketch of the necessary and sufficient conditions for the action. No historian can give a complete account of such conditions; to do so would require an impossible mass of detail. The reader does not really require such details to understand the action. Bancroft does not need to describe all the physical, chemical, and biological laws involved when one soldier shoots another, nor does he need to describe minutely the terrain through which an army passes. Such details are given only when they are required to render the events of the action more probable or plausible in the mind of the reader. If the army's march has been impeded by a swollen river, the historian may need to tell us so in order to justify the army's delay in reaching its objectives. If a character (or colony) has rebelled against authority at some earlier point, a later rebellion may seem more plausible to the reader, even if no direct connection can be drawn between the two events. Congruency of ideas may also be appealed to: in effect, Bancroft argues that the Puritan emphasis on freedom of conscience rendered the development of American democracy more probable, though he does not feel bound to trace a direct link between the Puritan dogma and particular events.

But not all of the scenic material can be explained as contributing to the probability of the narrative action. Some of it is present to help see the action in a wider context—an anecdote may illuminate a historical character as a human being without affecting the sequence of events in which he plays a part. From Bancroft's standpoint, William Penn's slaveholding is an anomaly, not a facet of his character which decisively affected the course of history; but he still records it. The historian's commitment to the reality of the past will lead him to include such scenic material, when literary critics might regard it as non-functional. In fact, it does serve an important function, that of maintaining the credibility of the historian as narrator: Bancroft's willingness to admit that a sympathetic character held slaves may reassure us about his objectivity. Even trivial details—the color of a man's eyes, for example—contribute to our sense that the author's research has aimed at recovering the reality of the past. Only large works, like Bancroft's, can support many such details just for the heightened realism they add—even as only a *Moby Dick* can support the cetological chapters.

Finally, we should note that the author may use scenic details to help shape our reactions to events. That Penn was devoted to his wife and children is even less relevant to his public career than his slaveholding, yet Bancroft, who wishes us to think well of Penn, takes time to tell us of Penn's domestic virtues. In the next chapter, we will discuss this use of detail at greater length.[5]

Like most literary terms, "scene" and "scenic" are simply more or less useful analytic tools that exist in the mind of the critic, not in the work. What we choose to consider as "scenic" in Bancroft's history depends on what we consider the artistic whole of the work to be. Most of the volumes can be considered artistic wholes in themselves; we have seen that they often end with a passage of reflection rounding off the story to date. The first unit of the *History*, the "History of the Colonization," can also be considered an artistic whole. Or we may choose to treat the ten-volume sequence as a single work. In other words, the unity of the *History* is additive and cumulative. A literary parallel would be a lyric sequence in which the first lyric is published separately, then given new meaning by a matching second lyric, and so on; an example would be T. S. Eliot's *Four Quartets*.

Within each of the books discussed so far there are elements which are purely scenic from the point of view of that volume or its unit. In the perspective afforded by the last four volumes of the original ten, the bulk of the first six volumes are scenic. The last four volumes deal with the Revolution and its immediate antecedents, and their addition to the total work makes the central action of the whole sequence the Revolution; for the previous volumes are now seen as discussing events which paved the way for the Revolution. The reader may now perceive a new significance in words quoted earlier—"The period through which we have passed shows why we are a free people; the coming period will show why we are a united people" (II, 466). The first two units of the *History* are thus seen as providing, first, the freedom, which made the growth of the revolutionary spirit possible, and, second, the unity which made possible the successful conduct of the Revolution. If the Revolution is the central aspect of the work as a whole, the specific events described in the earlier volumes are not essential links in the narrative, but their overall effect is required to establish the probability of the Revolution.

Volume I may provide a convenient example of the importance of the size of the unit considered. Volume I announces itself as the first in a series of volumes, but it was published separately; and, as the first work in his history Bancroft shaped it carefully. It by no means completes the history of the colonization, and yet it has a certain internal unity of its own. What this unity is should be obvious from even a brief perusal of the chapter headings which follow its introduction: "Early Voyages–French Settlements"; "Spaniards in the United States"; "England Takes Possession of the United States"; "Colonization of Virginia"; "Slavery"; "Dissolution of the London Company"; "Restrictions on Colonial Commerce"; "Colonization of Maryland"; "The Pilgrims"; "Extended Colonization of New England"; "The United Colonies of New England." Although the colonizing efforts of other nations are touched upon in the first three chapters, the title and the space assigned indicate from the beginning that the concern of the volume is with the English efforts and with those English colonies in the New World which later became the United States.

The main narrative line of the volume is the story of the first English colonies in America. The history of New Netherlands, which begins well within the temporal confines of this volume, is reserved for Volume II–for the time when its history becomes entwined with and then part of the history of the English colonies. Volume I contains accounts of the first Spanish and French efforts in America because the early voyages provide the necessary preconditions of the English settlements, even though they are not directly in the chain of events dealing with those settlements; again, in terms of narrative structure, this account serves a passive scenic function. The Spanish and French discoveries may also be considered as important because through them New World shores first impinged on the English imagination. Bancroft accordingly devotes as much time to Cabot as to Columbus, for the Spanish and French settlements which followed provide the context for English action and (a factorial function) the stimulus of that action.

The line dealing with English colonization may be said to begin with the fourth chapter, "England Takes Possession of the United States." The method is to discuss the various settlements and carry forward their history to the time of the Puritan Revolution, an external event affecting them all. After a survey of the first efforts, three chapters concentrate on Virginia. Maryland, whose history is closely bound to that of Virginia, is granted the next chapter; and the last chapters tell of the colonization of New England. The New England colonies are seen as adding a tradition of popular democracy to the practice of popular sovereignty found in the two Southern colonies. The chapters devoted to them are thus more detailed (over forty per cent of the volume) and form an appropriate climax to the volume thematically. The New England colonies are seen as the goal toward which the historic process was moving in the earlier efforts of Old England to establish colonies. But if the concluding chapter, summarizing the state of the New England colonies on the eve of the Restoration, is an appropriate form of closure for the first volume, it illustrates at the same time the scenic character of the volume in relation to the rest of the *History*. Its concluding pages on the nature of puritanism sum up the political implications of the establishment of Puritan colonies in America. Bancroft's insistence on the link between Puritanism and democratic ideals stresses the elements in Puritanism which make possible the role of the Puritans' descendants in the American Revolution.

Naturally, a great deal of expository information of the sort found in these passages can be conveyed in the interstices of a narrative. The large scale of Bancroft's design enables him to pause for larger blocks of exposition without materially affecting the flow of his narrative. Another example of material scenic in its function within the smaller unit of structure would be Chapter VI of Volume IV, a survey of conditions in "The Old Thirteen Colonies" in 1754. This chapter is not, however, a simple review of all that Bancroft could tell the reader about the life of these colonies at that point in history—the sort of survey best seen in well known examples by Thomas Macaulay and Henry Adams. Scenic in interest, Bancroft's material is carefully subordinated to the narrative of which it is a part. It is designed to explain what would lead the colonists to resist tighter controls by London: the Southern colonies' tradition of self-government is again touched upon; the growing union of the American colonies, the theme of the unit (Volumes IV-VI) is anticipated in a remark that New York's geographical "position invited it to foster American union" (IV, 144). The account of the New England colonies again emphasizes the social implications of the Reformed tradition.

A final example of scenic structure within these first six volumes is the first four chapters of Volume V: the first is a general survey of "The Continent of Europe, 1763"; the second discusses France in 1763; the third and fourth chapters discuss "England and its Dependencies" in the same year. The chapters on the situation in England obviously prepare for the conflict between the colonies and England; most of this volume tells the story with the focus on English politics. The chapters on the Continental powers provide the context for British statesmanship and summarize the state of international affairs at the conclusion of the Seven Years' War, which is dealt with in the previous volume. The relevance of these chapters is thus tangential at best, which is no doubt why Bancroft eventually eliminated them.

Chapters on the characteristics of the American colonies and of the European powers obviously serve a scenic function in the *History* as a whole as well as in the unit of it in which they appear. More important is the scenic function of the first six volumes for the complete *History*: the three volumes covering the colonial period deal with a subject worthwhile in itself, but it is also the story of "why we are a free people." A briefer account of the Revolution would require a briefer account of the people who made it; indeed, only an account as detailed as Bancroft's could sustain the weight of background provided. We might, for example, simply survey the temper of the people and the character of their institutions at some point—1763, 1774, or whatever point the historian chooses to begin his narrative. A brief account of the Revolution, even written from Bancroft's point of view, could surely afford no more than this without having a top-heavy structure. Bancroft can afford the added details which come with an attempt to trace the development of the national psychology and institutions. Moreover, his own historical style seems always to have moved him to seek out genetic explanations. Not only must we seek New England's philosophy by looking to its Puritan origins, but we must explain the Puritans by tracing the history of the Reformation. Bancroft's flirtation with the notion of inherent Anglo-Saxon love of law or with the Teutonic origins of democracy is probably best explained as another example of this propensity.

In the context of the *History* as a whole, the period of colonization does not occupy an excessive amount of space. Three volumes cover the history of the colonies from 1492 to 1748; three more volumes take the story to 1774; the last four volumes cover the years to 1782. The increasingly detailed account may have been dictated in part by the availability of materials, but it also corresponds to the focus of interest on the climax of the work's action—the great events of the Revolutionary War. The more detailed treatment of later events is not, moreover, the only indication that the earlier volumes are to be taken as background for the later; within the context of the complete *History*, Bancroft's concentration on the issues of popular sovereignty and democratic liberty, although explanable as a product of his own deepest convictions about history and politics, can be seen at work as thematic unifiers.

The elements which Bancroft seizes on as significant in the history of the first colonies are those which look forward to the Revolution; with the complete *History* before us, this is justified not simply by a "presentist" philosophy of history but also by the requirements of his narrative. "Why we are a free people" is important because the colonists are soon to be depicted as a free people driven to seek independence in order to continue to enjoy their freedom. The result gives coherence to the *History*. It is true that certain aspects of the colonization process are neglected in Bancroft's story, but this is at least partly inevitable—"Any selection of reality must, in certain circumstances, function as a *deflection* of reality. ... In its selectivity, it is a reduction."[6] Only an unduly reductionist philosophy of history could condemn Bancroft for a failure to do what he did not set out to do; from the beginning he seems to have seen the history of the colonization as a prelude to the achievement of freedom. The relevant question is, therefore, how well his volumes about the colonizing process contribute to our understanding of what made the Revolution possible.

The next three volumes, as they approach the events of the Revolution itself, are more closely connected to it. Indeed, Bancroft sees the Revolution as having its source in the events following 1748; he seems to believe that the struggle had become inevitable by 1774: "As the fleets and armies of England went forth to consolidate arbitrary power, the sound of war everywhere else on the earth died away. Kings sat still in awe, and nations turned to watch the issue" (VI, 528). The sixth volume "completes" the account of the "causes" of the American Revolution (VI, iii). The second unit of the *History* may thus be said to cover the "ultimate" or "underlying" causes of the conflict, but the climactic chain of events in the *History* as a narrative begins with the immediate sources of the Revolution and proceeds with the account of the conflict itself, if we view the *History* from the perspective of these last volumes.

The most important of these underlying factors is pointed to by Bancroft's "the coming period will show why we are a united people." Bancroft's emphasis on union in the second unit (published in the 1850s) may have been influenced by his knowledge of the forces threatening to split apart the federal union over the slavery question. But this theme, too, is an important support to the narrative structure. The Continental Congress did not spring into being without previous preparation for the idea of an American union. Bancroft characteristically opens the unit with an appeal to the general law of the unity of the race, telling us that "To have asserted clearly the union of mankind was the distinctive glory of the Christian religion" (IV, 7). He soon points out that at the beginning of the tale the thirteen colonies were still more closely bound to the mother country than to each other, but he has provided the ideological framework for their final adhesion. The approach of the French and Indian War helped Americans become "familiar with the thought of joining from their own free choice in one confederacy" (IV, 92). Benjamin Franklin's plan for union (1754), although it failed to win approval, helped give concrete shape to the idea. At the time, however, America was not yet prepared for the step; and "reflecting men in England dreaded American union as the keystone of independence" (IV, 126).

Another structural factor in conveying the feeling of the growing unity of the colonies is Bancroft's focus, especially in Volume IV, on the activities of the British Parliament. The first three volumes had concentrated on actions in the separate colonies; as seen from London, the colonies naturally appear more of a single entity. Many of the chapters dealing with developments in America report the reaction of colonists to actions aimed at the colonies as a group. By mingling quotations from one colony with those from another, Bancroft demonstrates a growing intellectual agreement in a way that anticipates the coming political union. The resistance to the Stamp Act marked "The Day Star of the American Union" (V, Chapter XIII). The heroes of what follows are Samuel Adams in Massachusetts and Benjamin Franklin in London, the steadfast advocates of colonial cooperation. The non-importation agreements are treated as another sign of growing union, despite their eventual failure; the bills to punish Massachusetts bring forth additional signs of the united will of the colonies—"the union was perfect" (VI, 525). The stage was prepared for the drama of independence.

To speak of these volumes as scenic in function is not to deny that they contain narrative lines of action or even that those actions may be, particularly in the second unit, the source of unity at the level of the unit; to so speak of them merely identifies their function within the larger work. And to speak of these scenic elements as subordinated to a narrative action is to speak only from a literary standpoint; historical explanation, as opposed to pure narrative, may well regard the presentation of underlying causes as more significant. Moreover, it should be clear that scenic elements may provide the artistic unity of a historical work, as they do when Volume I is considered by itself.

II   *"Plot" in Bancroft's Narrative*

A historian who, like Bancroft, believed that the American experience demonstrated the inevitable progress of the human spirit might choose to convey this image of the past in a thematically organized story, showing progress in different areas of experience. Bancroft, however, chooses to construct a narrative action, a plot with a beginning, middle, and end. The thematically organized book would present us with a series of beginnings and endings; it might be an argument that the endings were superior to the beginnings. Bancroft's history has a plot because it provides the middle which shows how we got from the beginning to the end. The end of the ten-volume *History* is the achievement of American independence, and its purpose is to recount the events which led to that end, becinning with the discovery of the continent. If we choose to look at the last four volumes as a narrative unit, they begin in 1774, when "The penal acts of 1774 dissolved the moral connection between the two countries, and began the civil war" (VI, iii)—and by choosing these two acts as a starting point, Bancroft manages to place the blame for initiating hostilities on Britain. The dramatic center of this unit is the Declaration of Independence, with which Bancroft ends Volume VIII.

To call such a narrative action a "plot" also implies that it conforms to one of a limited number of archetypal patterns into which man has formed his experience. Given Bancroft's patriotism and meliorism, it is no surprise to find that his *History* does not exhibit the rise and fall of a complex tragic plot with a dramatic peripety. It should be clear, however, that this is a true narrative choice, although one made inevitable by Bancroft's ideological predispositions. Another historian might, for example, choose to make England the dramatic protagonist and tell how she won the continent with her victory in the Seven Years' War and then threw away the benefits of that great victory: "England became not so much the possessor of the Valley of the West, as the transient trustee, commissioned to transfer it from the France of the Middle Ages to the free people, who were making for humanity a new existence in America" (IV, 462). Such a story would focus on the partial disintegration of a social system, the net decline in the fortunes of a nation; the outlines of this approach are, in fact, to be found in the work of the so-called Imperial school, particularly in that of Lawrence H. Gipson. Compared with that of Bancroft, such a plot would be ironic or tragic; Bancroft's own plot is like that which Northrop Frye lists as the third of his "phases'. of comedy, the phase in which a new and better society comes to maturity and triumphs—like Frye's "action of comedy," Bancroft's *History* "moves from law to liberty."[7]

Although the Americans suffer a number of reverses in the war, the basic line of this progress from law to liberty is a simple upward thrust with no lasting reversals of fortune. If we take the total *History* as our unit of analysis, the action begins with the Puritans fleeing the laws governing religion in England; if we look at the last four volumes as a unit, the action begins with the colonies reacting against the Penal Laws by coming together in the Continental Congress. Within the four-volume unit, the Declaration of Independence is well placed at the center, for it marks the transition from law to liberty and divides the two years of preparation from the *agon* itself. The peace is an unambiguous and appropriate end to the action: English efforts to impose or retain the rule of Parliamentary law in the colonies have failed and liberty is won; a new and superior society has come to manhood in the community of nations, a society whose states "possessed beyond any other portion of the world the great ideas of their age, and enjoyed the practice of them by individual man in uncontrolled faith and industry, thought and action" (X, 592).

If Bancroft shapes his story so that it begins in law and ends in liberty, his plot provides the connecting middle by arranging events in lines of action in which one event follows another in a manner which the reader will accept as probable and intelligible. These lines of action create the unity and form of the *History*. Even within the main lines of action, we may distinguish certain incidents which are more important, more essential, than others. These are incidents which could not be altered without altering the effect of the whole. If we are telling the story of a military campaign, any decisive battle would be such an incident; although the armies' march to that battle would form part of the same line of action, the details of the route of march might have no effect on the outcome of the battle or the campaign. Like the incidents we have earlier termed "scenic," the details of the armies' march appear in the historian's actual narrative only when they contribute to the probability of the more essential events. Which incidents are regarded as essential depends on what story the historian has decided to tell and how he has decided to shape it; in a history of American painting, the Revolution itself might not appear as an essential incident. When historians covering roughly the same subject (like the Revolution) treat different events as essential, the difference is sometimes treated by historiographers as a result of opposed views of the "causes" of the

Revolution; it might equally well be seen as resulting from differing choices of overall narrative form.[8]

Bancroft's lines of action are, therefore, chains of contingent events linking together such essential incidents as the choice of Washington as commander in chief of the Continental Army, the central event of Chapter XXXVII in Volume VII. Obviously more than one line of action is involved, for the events of the American revolution could scarcely be fitted into one line. Such a subject poses special problems for the historian since the story involves characters little-known to one another acting in widely separated places, and the common relevance of their actions is established only by the common end to which they point. At least two basic dispositions of such material were available to Bancroft: he could choose to observe unity of time, placing together all events occurring at roughly the same time and arranging the whole in chronological order; or he could choose to observe unity of place, linking together events occurring in roughly the same geographical area and treating each area separately. If we seek to distinguish observable lines of action, a purely military history is likely to be organized on geographical lines, while a purely diplomatic history is more apt to follow chronological developments. In the first case, the opposing agents are armies and military leaders; in the second, nations. Bancroft's account includes both elements, but his inclusion of the diplomatic context of military action leads him to phrase the opposing agents as the "people" of the United States and the "government" of Great Britain—that is, a nation in the process of realizing itself versus a mere faction of the ruling class.

The volumes of the *History* generally cover chronological units, although there is a certain amount of overlapping, as between the first two volumes, in which the processes of colonization are discussed in terms of geographical units, because Bancroft chose to focus on internal developments at the expense of the central authority of Parliament. Within the volumes in general, even the later ones, a geographical arrangement often dominates. A less detailed account might permit a chronological arrangement using collective entities, the colonies versus Britain; although this opposition is central to Bancroft's history, his leisurely pace allows him to write at length about the internal arrangements of both sides. The result is that, in Bancroft's narrative, the British and Americans remain separate sets of characters in largely separate scenes, that is, there are independent lines of action. Even so, the essential events of any narrative are likely to be those in which such independent lines of action converge, and the most crucial events in Bancroft are those which mark the convergence of lines of action or lines of action representing the two great sides—the great battles of the war and the peace itself.

On the British side, the last four volumes carry forward at least three separate lines of action—the government, the Parliamentary opposition, and the army commanders in America. The American side is in some ways more complex, for Bancroft must deal with the relative lack of central control and coordination of the American efforts. Since he gives more detail on the American side, Bancroft rarely treats a state as a collective agent, though, as we might expect, he sometimes writes of the "people" of a state as speaking through their representatives. The initial distinguishing of separate lines of action is therefore primarily geographical—the thirteen colonies being treated as separate geographical entities. The earliest essential events within Volume VII are produced by the convergence of lines of action within the American side: the formation of the Continental Congress, the Second Continental Congress, and the decision to create a Continental Army. Thereafter, the divisions within the American side are smaller in number, though still geographical in design—the Congress itself, the army (in turn, considered by geographical area), and the American diplomats at work in Europe.[9] Although such internal divisions are based on historical reality, Bancroft's use of them is clearly affected by his decision to provide a detailed account and by the point of view he adopts. For example, his decision to treat the military history of the war from an American standpoint means that geographically separate campaigns are given a more separate treatment than might have been required had Bancroft approached the same battles from the standpoint of British strategy, which was more unified in conception, though sometimes impractical and often badly executed.

Although we have seen that the amount of detail given by Bancroft is a factor in determining the arrangement of lines of action, it should be remembered that Bancroft is engaged throughout in a continuous process of selection. His "plot" provides a principle of selection by highlighting certain essential incidents. The other incidents which comprise his lines of action are shown only as needed to provide continuity and to establish the probability of his essential events; we have earlier seen that "scenic" material is also subordinated to the demands of the plot, appearing only as it contributes to the probability of its action and our understanding of its meaning. Bancroft does not always maintain full control of this careful balancing act, and he sometimes lets his mastery of materials lead him into a disproportionate emphasis on a given subject—indeed, many of his later revisions aimed at pruning such excesses. But so massive a work can bear a few digressions, and Bancroft's vision of a free people coming together to win independence is powerful enough to provide a unified structure, within which his various lines of action and other material are usually kept in proper balance. Bancroft's mastery of other aspects of narrative technique—his construction of vivid episodes or his sometimes memorable style—would have won him less honor had they not been reinforced by the power of a clear narrative plot.

III   *"Character" in Bancroft's Narrative*

In biographies, characters may provide the unity of the work; in some narrative histories, small groups of characters serve the same function. But in Bancroft's work, as we have seen, the agents are subordinated to the actions in which they take part. Only occasionally does Bancroft allow a character to play any other role. When he does so, it is usually to allow a character to point to the meaning of events, a "scenic" function usually performed by Bancroft as narrator. Jonathan Edwards, for example, is credited with a recognition of the desirability of change in human affairs and the inevitability of progress: " 'The new creation'—such are his words—'is more excellent than the old. So it ever is, that when one thing is removed by God to make way for another, the new excels the old' " (III, 399). But allowing a character to point to a central theme of the work is not the same as developing that character for its own sake. The *History* has a large cast of characters, but very few of them are presented as fully rounded human beings.

Bancroft's history, detailed as it is, covers too wide a scope, too long a stretch of time for any single set of agents to be crucial in its action. This is an esthetic disadvantage, for much of our interest in the actions of fiction and drama depends on our involvement in the fates of particular characters toward whom we are sympathetic or unsympathetic; and much of the significance of these actions depends upon the moral qualities of particular characters. In a narrative history like Bancroft's, other sources of interest must be found; and this need accounts for the reader popularity of histories dealing with events of intrinsic interest, whether because of the seriousness of the consequences, national (the Civil War) or personal (crime), or because of the emotions involved (love and sex). Bancroft certainly has a subject of

great seriousness, the founding of a nation; and he has likewise the
natural interest of a people in its own history. He loses no opportunity
to point out the worldwide consequences of his story or the influence of
the American past upon the American present. But he also seeks to
provide his narrative with a few of the advantages which derive from
the readers' interest in and understanding of important characters.
Since he cannot deal with many characters at length without throwing
his narrative action out of balance, the traditional functions of
"character" are served in the *History* by a handful of hero-figures, by
the use of representative characters, and by recourse to personified
groups.[10]

When we speak of heroes in history, we speak of villains as well;
what distinguishes "great men" in a work like the *History* is that they
are presented as being in important respects independent of their
environment, able to mold it by their acts. For Bancroft, this
independence does not reduce history to chance; in Bancroft's teleological framework, history is guided by Providence, but its historical
inevitability can manifest itself in individual men. Bancroft's heroes
may represent their class or society, but they are not merely
representative of it or conditioned by it. In the action, their behavior is
explained only partly in terms of external constraints and pressures;
much of the explanation is their own character, one God-given rather
than one shaped by circumstances. They stand and fall by their virtues
and their vices. Roger Williams and Pitt are sympathetic characters of
this sort in the *History*; Lord North and George III are less sympathetic
but no less independent. But the greatest representative of this class is
the true hero of the last four volumes, George Washington.

Washington's emergence as a hero is carefully prepared for. Even
before he becomes the American commander—and thus a full agent in
the action—he has received a certain amount of attention, one justified
by his eventual position more than by his youthful exploits. The
three volumes on the colonization process end with an allusion to the
young Washington that identifies him with the American wilderness as
opposed to the courts of Europe and with the strivings of the people as
opposed to the privileges of aristocracy:

At the very time of the congress of Aix la Chapelle, the woods of
Virginia sheltered the youthful George Washington, the son of a widow.
Born by the side of the Potomac, beneath the roof of a Westmoreland
farmer, almost from infancy his lot had been the lot of an orphan. . . .
And now, at sixteen years of age, in quest of an honest maintenance,

encountering intolerable toil; . . . this stripling surveyor in the woods, with no companion but his unlettered associates, contrasted strangely with the imperial magnificence of the congress of Aix la Chapelle. And yet God had selected, no Kaunitz, nor Newcastle, not a monarch of the house of Hapsburg, nor of Hanover, but the Virginia stripling, to give an impulse to human affairs, and, as far as events can depend on an individual, had placed the rights and the destinies of countless millions in the keeping of the widow's son. (III, 467-68)

The first appearance of Bancroft's Washington is, therefore, as a hero chosen to redeem his people. We might expect to be told next that Washington was fed in this wilderness by ravens, but the cautious historian in Bancroft peeps through to add the qualifying "as far as events can depend on an individual." Bancroft's heroes must ride to greatness by identifying with the will of the people. And, although Bancroft speaks of the will of God where a modern historian might refer to the ironies of history, the effect of the contrast he draws does not depend on his providential interpretation of its meaning; the will of Bancroft's God is seen as manifest in the outcome of the *History*, but He does not become an agent in its action.

Bancroft's account of Washington's participation in the colonial wars presents a sequence of anecdotes designed to bolster this heroic picture. The young Washington, "a pupil of the wilderness" (IV, 108-109), braves the dangers of winter and savages to report on French activity in the Ohio Valley. The skirmish at Great Meadows in 1754 (ten French killed, twenty-five wounded) is regarded as precipitating the great war which followed: " 'Fire!' said Washington, and, with his own musket, gave the example. That word of command kindled the world into flame. It was the signal for the first great war of revolution. . . . In repelling France from the basin of the Ohio, Washington broke the repose of mankind" (IV, 199). Bancroft here ignores the fact that Washington himself was soon forced to withdraw—and the failure of General Braddock's expedition the next year is laid at the door of the British regulars.

The account of the war which followed anticipates Washington's high destiny at a number of points; Bancroft rather encourages the reader to see Washington as under the special protection of Providence, although he is too cautious to say so himself. Great stress is laid on his valor in combat and on the remarkable failure of enemy marksmen to bring him down. Washington is quoted as giving the credit to God, and Bancroft allows "a learned divine" to speak of "that heroic youth,

Colonel Washington, whom I cannot but hope Providence has preserved in so signal a manner for some important service to his country" (IV, 190). When Washington returns home after the capture of Fort Duquesne, Bancroft notes that he has in his rooms busts of great men; and the only one of a living person is that of Frederic of Prussia— another nation-founder, another childless hero, father only to his country.

Washington does not play an important role in the events leading to the Revolution. Even among the Virginians, Bancroft devotes the most space to Patrick Henry, partly because of his real importance and partly because of Bancroft's own delight in the oratory of the various colonial legislatures. Washington remains in the background, but Bancroft notes that Patrick Henry considered him for his "solid information and sound judgment . . . the greatest man of them all" (VII, 153). Any full sketch of Washington's character as a mature man is reserved for the end of Volume VII when Washington is appointed commander in chief of the new Continental Army.

In this chapter in Volume VII Washington's early trials are once more rehearsed. His three years as a surveyor in the wilderness now assume the form of a Toynbee-like withdrawal-and-return, a communion with a higher power, in which "nature revealed to him her obedience to serene and silent law" (VII, 394). Now he was to become a law-giver in himself, one who brought goodness "to the camp and the cabinet, and established a new criterion of human greatness" (VII, 399). The highest kind of American, he goes beyond mere representativeness and takes on a mythical identity with his country: "the most complete expression of all its attainments and aspirations. He studied his country and conformed to it. His countrymen felt that he was the best type of America, and rejoiced in it, and were proud of it. They lived in his life, and made his success and his praise their own" (VII, 398). The religious tone of these phrases is more open in a reference to Washington's unequaled and "almost divine faculty to command the confidence of his fellow-men and rule the willing" (VII, 400). This account of Washington is followed by three short closing chapters on the Battle of Bunker Hill. Volume VII thus ends with the introduction of the great American general and the Army he was soon to command.

Bancroft's Washington is established for us as a character of weight and dignity, as one fit to play a heroic role in a drama of the greatest significance. When there is a serious conflict of opinion among the revolutionaries, or a clash of personalities, our sympathy is naturally extended to Washington. In each case, Bancroft argues the rightness of Washington's judgment, but he has prepared us to accept such arguments by his estimate of Washington's character. It is possible to see Washington as a great natural leader who became a fine general in the course of the Revolution, but Bancroft's Washington is wise in all things as if by nature's gift. As Washington comes to see the necessity for a single American nation, Bancroft uses this realization both as evidence of his wisdom and as an example of the way in which he embodied the collective wisdom of the people. Always in the background is the figure of Washington the Redeemer, the man sent by God to suffer for his people and to bring them to victory; the rhetoric sometimes reminds us that Bancroft had once thought to be a Unitarian minister:

The sharp tribulation which assayed his fortitude carried with it a divine and animating virtue. Hope and zeal illuminated his grief. His emotions come to us across the century like strains from that eternity which repairs all losses and rights all wrongs; in his untold sorrows, his trust in Providence kept up in his heart an under-song of wonderful sweetness. The spirit of the Most High dwells among the afflicted, rather than the prosperous; and he who has never broken his bread in tears knows not the heavenly powers. The trials of Washington are the dark, solemn ground on which the beautiful work of his country's salvation was embroidered. (IX, 218).

In Bancroft's *History*, Washington is a principal agent in one line of action and the greatest hero of the war. But even Washington is but one character among many. We are told only so much about him as is needed to convey Bancroft's high conception of his character and abilities or to explain his actions in events of historical interest; even in dealing with the Father of His Country, Bancroft indulges in few digressions; he does not discuss Washington for his own sake but as he affects the narrative action. Washington is not on the scene of many of the most important battles of the Revolution, and he plays no part in the diplomatic maneuverings leading to French recognition and to the final peace. For these there are other heroes, other villains. Of these other figures, the one whose stature most nearly approaches that of Washington is Benjamin Franklin, who, first seen as a young apprentice in Volume III, is later dealt with as the proposer of the Albany Plan of Union, and is at last presented as the one man whose presence helps unify the long series of negotiations leading to independence and peace.

Franklin, however, was too clever a politician to inspire Bancroft to the religious rhetoric which surrounds his Washington.

Washington and Franklin are both representative and individualized characters. But there are a number of minor characters whose importance as agents in the action does not justify their being given much individual character but who are given a representative function, rather like a minor character in fiction or drama, who may be a barely individualized stock type representing a given attitude or profession. In this category we may place the seven men who died at Lexington: "village heroes, who were more than of noble blood, proving by their spirit that they were of a race divine. They gave their lives in testimony to the rights of mankind, bequeathing to their country an assurance of success in the mighty struggle which they began. . . . They fulfilled their duty not from the accidental impulse of the moment; their action was the slowly ripened fruit of Providence and of time" (VII, 294, 295).

The time and place of their death make these men significant, rather than any power over the course of events which they exerted as individuals. Because they are the first fallen, they are representative; and because the details of death make an individual's death important where a number (seven dead) might seem insignificant, Bancroft tells how each dies, in sometimes moving phrases. For example, "Jonathan Harrington, junior, was struck in front of his own house on the north of the common. His wife was at the window as he fell. With the blood rushing from his breast, he rose in her sight, tottered, fell again, then crawled on hands and knees towards his dwelling; she ran to meet him, but only reached him as he expired on their threshold" (VII, 294).

That minor characters should be assigned a representative function, that heroes themselves should serve so, should be no surprise if we recall that Bancroft's *History* is concerned with the fate of nations rather than with that of individuals. Out of this emphasis arises the tendency to treat individuals as emblems of nations and as social groups and also to speak of personified groups, assigning to them those moral qualities which more cautious historians reserve for individuals. As we have seen, personification is common in Bancroft, whose faith in the popular will often expressed itself in the assumption that resolutions taken by legislative bodies express the general will of the people: "The people of Maryland . . . acted with moderation and humanity. . . . In May and the early part of June, the people, in county meetings, renounced the hope of reconciliation" (VIII, 447).

Abroad, Bancroft deals with other such personified groups—the nobility of France, the factions of the British parliament, the courtiers of Spain. Groups of this sort, although they may play the role of characters in an action, are not subject by nature to moral judgment as is an individual character. But if it is such evaluations that produce our pleasure or pain at the fortunes of a character, Bancroft's willingness to ascribe moral qualities to collectivities may be a literary strength, even if it would seem to impair the professional objectivity of his history. The largest entity to be consistently treated as such in the *History* is, of course, the American people, whose essential agreement is stressed while the divisions in the English parliament are treated as basic. This faith in the people has its source in Bancroft's political beliefs, but it has a literary effect since only the American people as a people can serve as a unifying agent for the total action of the *History*.

CHAPTER 4

Narrative Manner

EVEN in academia, ours has become an age of abridgments; soon we shall read more abstracts than articles, and already we introduce our graduate students to our predecessors by way of selected readings; meanwhile, popular works of fiction and nonfiction grow smaller while costing more.[1] We need not, however, imagine that even a nineteenth-century gentleman of leisure was necessarily pleased with the length and stately pace of Bancroft's *History*. In 1860, one such man wrote in his diary that Bancroft's latest volume was "poor stuff, filled with unnecessary details, without just thought, interesting narrative or breadth of effect, commonplace, vulgar in feeling, factitious in sentiment, weak, tawdry & diffuse in style. A miserable performance, truly. The 7th vol. is out and he has only got to the Declaration of Independence. He spins it out because he sells it by the volume. It may be useful as a book of reference, but for nothing else. The history of the Revolution is yet to be written."[2]

The charge of "unnecessary details" brings us to another level of narrative choices: the tactical as opposed to the strategic considerations dealt with in the previous chapters. These choices are not less important ones, although they are narrower in their scope. Plot, thought, and character are generalized attributes of literature; the distinctiveness and much of the virtue of "narrative," as opposed to drama or lyric poetry, lies in its method of presentation and in the use of the narrative voice. This chapter focuses, therefore, on Bancroft's construction of episodes, first as seen in one of the *History*'s most effective sections, where we have available his early drafts, and later as seen in his *History of the Formation of the Constitution* (1882).[3] This work, published separately from the *History* though later incorporated in the "Author's Last Revision," would seem less open to the charge of unnecessary detail since its two volumes take us from the end of the war to the inauguration of Washington in five hundred and fifty pages of narrative, although another three hundred and fifty pages of appended letters and papers add to the bulk of the volumes. This narrative obviously has a more rapid pace and greater compression than that of the later volumes of the *History*; indeed, Bancroft himself assures us that he has "spared no pains to compress the narrative within the narrowest limits consistent with clearness" (I, xvi). Because it is a separate work, it also deserves to be considered as a narrative synthesis in its own right.

I   *Incident and Episode: Lexington and Concord*

The seventh volume of the *History* may have impressed our diarist as a "miserable performance," but many have thought it contained some of Bancroft's best writing. These were the glory days of the Revolution; of all of them, April 19, 1775, when the minute men of Lexington and Concord faced a British raiding party, presented the most heroic subject for Bancroft's prose, a prose best suited to the praise of heroes. In his abridgment of Bancroft's *History* (Chicago, 1966), Russel B. Nye has termed these chapters "unmatched anywhere else in Bancroft's writings" (151). Bancroft's drafts show that he had worked hard to achieve this effect.[4]

Historians cannot rely on inspiration since the Muse is apt to forget whether it was Balboa or Cortez who stood and gazed at the Pacific; the magnitude of Bancroft's undertaking made it particularly necessary for him to proceed systematically. His notes, taken from both original documents and published sources, were carefully arranged and classified in notebooks with both a day-by-day and a topical listing. Arranging his notes was an exhausting and tedious part of his task but worth the effort. They had been taken over a long period of years and, in later years, sometimes by paid copyists. They had to be organized before they could be used. As he grew older and richer, Bancroft was able to use trained assistants for some of this work as well.

Bancroft returned from his service in England in August, 1849, and set to work on his volumes dealing with the Revolutionary Era; volumes IV and V were published in 1852, and three more volumes appeared in 1856, 1858, and 1860. As he set to work, he had at hand two possible outlines of the work before him. One included the already accomplished colonial volumes in a five-part outline: Colonial America, Insurgent America, Independent America, Victorious America, and United America. The other, covering only the post-colonial period, also had five parts: The Over-Throw of the European Colonial System, How Great Britain Estranged America, Independence Declared, Independence Acknowledged (also listed as America Received among the Nations or as America takes its Place among the Nations), and Union (or Union Consolidated). The first four of these parts were to become the four "epochs" into which the last seven volumes of the *History* are divided; Bancroft was to deal with the consolidated Union in his *Constitution* volumes and complete the work of this outline by uniting them with the *History* in his "Author's Last Revision."

The third of these "epochs" is "America Declares Itself Independent." It takes up volumes VII and VIII in the published history, but notes headed "III. America Declares Independence" suggest that Bancroft had originally intended to dispose of this epoch in a single volume of eight chapters, including a single chapter for the events at Lexington and Concord:

I. King in Council. The British Aristocracy insults the Great American Plebian; and in parliament becomes a tyrant. 1774 January to May.
II. Congress of 1774. The Colonies in Congress resolve to resist.
III. Boston, the Martyr, ministered to. Winter of 1774-1775.
IV. Lexington and Concord. 19 April 1775.
V. Bunker Hill. May to June 1775.
VI. Siege of Boston.
VII. No more Kings. [men. in this chapter the negotiations with the German princes]
VIII. No more Colonial Dependence. May to July Fourth 1776.

This pattern is basically the one followed by the completed "Epoch Third." Bancroft's habit of slowing his pace as he came closer to the Revolution itself is seen again in his devoting one volume (VII) to the first five chapters of the above outline, reserving another whole volume (VIII) for the last three. A good part of the added bulk is consumed by material Bancroft had quarried from the archives of Europe, but some of it is taken up with a more detailed account of the background of the Declaration of Independence than Bancroft seems at first to have envisaged. The general effect is to flesh out the British side of the approaching conflict. The negotiations for mercenaries, for example, occupy two full chapters for themselves—"How George the Third Fared in His Bid for Russians" (VIII, 144-56) and "Britain Engages Foreign Troops" (VIII, 250-71). Yet another plan of organization for this unit may be suggested by ten draft pages headed "Chapter VII: Lexington, Concord, and Bunker Hill." They begin: "The crisis was at hand. Parliament in the exercise of its power, had been entreated, remonstrated against, resisted. . . . At last a stern, unbending will in England, springing from the king himself, sustained especially by Bute, Mansfield and North, was bent on reducing the colonies to submission, and was met in America by a will as strong, springing from conviction, living in the people, enlightened by discussion, animated and enflamed by a love of freedom, a regard for consistency, and a boundless, illimitable hope." The draft begins with events of January, 1775, and, by its title, seems originally intended to cover the events which eventually comprised the entire last half of Volume VII.

Bancroft evidently maintained something of this last framework as he wrote the more detailed draft which was to form the basis of his final copy, for the notebook section which contains his first draft efforts on Lexington and Concord is headed "VII" throughout. Even the fair copy, which was either his last or next-to-last draft, was first titled "Chapter XXVIII: Lexington and Concord, April 19, 1775." The "and Concord" has been crossed out and that material relegated to Chapter XXIX, as it appears in the published volume. Typically, Bancroft chose to divide his manuscript, not upon the completion of the action at Lexington, but on a moral statement. Chapter XXIX thus begins with the British troops firing a volley in honor of their triumph at Lexington and then marching on toward Concord. Bancroft continued to think of the chapters together and makes one chapter of them again in his "Author's Last Revision."

The events of the day constitute a single natural episode in Bancroft's action—a British raiding party sets out after the rebel arms stored at Concord, is delayed at Lexington, searches without much success at Concord, and returns to Boston, under fire much of the way—and the events of the day were to have a single, important effect on public opinion in the colonies. The source of unity is the British effort, rather than the scattered and ill-coordinated efforts of the Americans; although giving as much attention as he can to the American preparations and actions, Bancroft simplifies his narrative by making the British his main line of action. If the result has found general favor, it may be partly because the event then forms a single coherent action in itself, a rising and falling action in which the British march out, triumph in Lexington, and then find themselves worsted on their return, until "a little after sunset, the survivors escaped across the Charlestown creek" (VII, 309).

From the British point of view, the affair began as a police action in which evasion was more to be feared than armed resistance, but the effect of Bancroft's selection and presentation of incidents is to make them armed aggressors. An example is his relatively greater concentration on the events at Lexington and the march on to Concord, at the expense of the British retreat, when most of the British losses were suffered. A concentration on the incidents at Lexington and Concord may have been dictated by the greater number of accounts available, by their greater internal unity of action, and by their important effect on the imagination of the colonials; the effect is to present the American slain as martyrs and the British slain as statistics.

Also important is Bancroft's insistence on fixing the blame upon the British for firing first; as one of those who had helped bring about the Mexican War, Bancroft knew that Americans felt more comfortable when assured that they were only defending themselves. Accounts of Lexington are particularly confused, but Bancroft's own grows more definite with each draft. His first lines at least refrain from definitely assigning responsibility among the British: "The commanders of the British troops, Col. Smith, Maj. Pitcairn, and (Clark) ride forward and bid the company disperse. The company stands silent and undaunted; without offense: stand as witnesses against aggression. The British troops are marching in [illegible]; the light infantry on the right; the grenadiers on the left. Pitcairn consulting ["consulting" is then crossed out] fired his pistol and commands his men to fire towards the militia; the foremost officer, who was within a few yards of our men, brandishing his sword, and then pointing towards them, with a loud voice said to the troops, 'Fire, by God, fire.' "

Interlinear revisions on the same page amplify the actions of the British officers and the motives of the Americans. Now the three British officers "ride forward on horseback to the front of the body, and when within five or six rods of the militia, one of them cries out, 'Ye villains, ye rebels, disperse, damn you, disperse.' " The company, still standing "without offense," is described in even more heroic terms: "they could not resist: they would not fly. They were determined not to begin hostilities, yet not to yield rights. Upon no consideration whatever would they begin the scenes of blood." A note on the opposite leaf, the back of the previous draft page, shows that Bancroft remained unclear and knew it: "One of the three officers, whether the same or not is not easy determined, said, 'Lay down your arms, damn you, why do you not lay down your arms.' "

By the time of the fair copy, Pitcairn has been singled out as the major villain: "Pitcairn rode forward, and when within five or six rods of them, cried out 'Disperse, ye villains, ye rebels, disperse; lay down your arms; why don't you lay down your arms and disperse.' The main part of the company stood motionless in their place, witnesses against aggression; too few to resist, too brave to fly. At this Pitcairn discharged a Pistol, and with a loud voice cried 'Fire.' " This version is pretty much the published passage: an interlinear notation changes "in their place" to the more military "in their ranks"; on the way to the printers, the American "company" became the patriotic "countrymen," Pitcairn's question acquires a question mark, and his pistol loses its capital letter.

The changes between the original and the fair copy are instructive. They are by no means all in the same direction. The singling out of Pitcairn and the collapsing and partial rewriting of quotations are certainly questionable. On the other hand, the bravery of the Americans is expressed somewhat more cautiously with the alteration of "The company stands silent and undaunted" to "The main part of the company stood motionless." The rhetoric is somewhat more restrained and perhaps more effective because of the elimination of "without offense" and the interlinear comments on the unwillingness of the Americans to commence hostilities. Other changes seem more purely stylistic: the repetition of "company" in the rough draft becomes "them" and "company" in the fair copy, but is elevated to "minute men" and "countrymen" in the published version. The cliché of a brandished sword is omitted; and the exact disposition of the British troops, not relevant in this incident, is gone. Both the questionable and the acceptable alterations make the passage shorter and more definite.

The successive drafts of the Lexington chapter show that Bancroft was concerned to condense his narrative both by eliminating unnecessary details and by finding more succinct expressions. That he was led to this in good part by a concern for narrative effectiveness seems obvious; for reducing total wordage can hardly have been his aim since he expands upon his narrative base with the rhetorical excursions which take up about twenty-five per cent of the chapter.

The first few pages of the rough draft of this chapter are in a particularly disorganized state, as Bancroft struggled with materials from various sources and looked for a way to tie together the separate British and American preparations. In the end, the first three paragraphs move back and forth between the British effort to maintain secrecy and the American effort to secure warning. This opening leads naturally to the riders who gave alarm, the most famous being Paul Revere. Separate paragraphs give glimpses of the receipt of the alarm and the mustering of the minute-men at Concord and Acton; several more paragraphs are then devoted to Lexington and to the men who gathered there, thereby setting the stage for the confrontation which is the chapter's climax.

The opening sentences of the draft run: "On the fifteen of April, the day of the adjournment of the Provincial Congress, General Gage, who, by his spies had obtained a report of the state of the country and the amount of stores, collected at Worchester and conquered, prepared for an expedition into the country to destroy the stores collected at Concord. The expedition was got ready with all the secrecy in his power." A note follows giving sources for the soldiers taken off duty. In the fair copy, this passage is condensed into one more specific sentence: "On the afternoon of the day on which the Provincial Congress of Massachusetts adjourned, Gage gave orders for taking the light infantry and grenadiers off duty, and secretly prepared an expedition to destroy the colony's stores at Concord." The addition of "of Massachusetts" is presumably to prevent confusion of the provincial body with the Continental Congress—in the draft, Bancroft himself had started to write "Continental Cong" before correcting himself—but the addition of the state name helps give a pleasing sense of closure to final reference to the "colony's stores." While the fair copy was still in his hands, Bancroft decided that "gave orders for taking" said no more than "took" and revised accordingly. No other substantive changes were made before publication.

The main lines of the draft of the confrontation at Lexington is a collection of separate facts put in a rough order with no more general reflections than occurred to Bancroft as he wrote. These reflections are amplified, and new thoughts added, on the facing page and yet again in the fair copy. An account of the Americans' silent wait has prefaced to it on the opposite page a couple of sentences on the pattern of "How often in that house they had heard God appealed to as the guardian of their fathers, the protector of their liberties!" In the fair copy, after one correction, this sentence emerges as "How often in that building they had with renewed professions of godliness, looked up to God as the stay of their fathers, and the protector of their liberties." Eventually, "godliness" was changed to "their faith" (on the pattern of "their fathers"), and "liberties" became "privileges," a word less expressive of Bancroft's political theory but alliterating with "protector."

As we saw in an earlier chapter of this study, Bancroft deliberately gives the details of the deaths of the seven men who were killed at Lexington. The rough draft contains only the facts, sometimes with notes on his source; the fair copy polishes the telling and adds a paragraph pointing the contrast between the dead, "crying unto God for vengeance from the ground," and the spring dawn—"Day came in all the beauty and warmth of early spring. The trees were budding" and so on. Additional reflection on early spring mornings evidently led Bancroft to eliminate the "and warmth" from the passage when published. The passage is presumably intended to place the reader in sympathy with the colonies' move to avenge these deaths. The next paragraph expands a few sentences praising the "rustic heroes" before whom the "centuries bowed themselves" to a page-long attribution of "the light that led them on" to a combined heritage from the Hebrews; from Greece and Rome; from Christ; from medieval Christianity; from Germanic and Anglo-Saxon traditions; from Martin Luther; from St. Paul, Augustine, and Calvin; from British and American Puritans; from the Glorious Revolution; from eighteenth-century liberalism; and from other unnamed proclaimers of "the reality and the rightfulness of human freedom." The chapter ends with Samuel Adams's prophetic recognition of the significance of the morning's events.

By the time Bancroft reached the Concord sections of his draft, he was writing more freely. Although the facing pages are full of possible additions, the language of his first draft is more like his published prose and less like the random notes than in the Lexington sections. The chapter moves easily, in the fair copy, between the British forces and the gathering Americans; the portion covering the British march back to Boston maintains its focus on the British. Most of the expansion between Bancroft's first lines and the fair copy is added narrative detail rather than reflection and exhortation.

Many of the changes made between the draft and copy are, however, designed to sway the reader's emotions: in line with Bancroft's general interpretation of the day's events, the relatively neutral "At first the British retreated in order" becomes, by a correction made on the fair copy, the pejorative "At first the invaders retreated in order"—later changed to "moved," probably from doubt whether it could yet be fairly described as a retreat. Passages which seem to be new in the fair copy portray the retreating British as descending to wanton plunder and "savage cruelty." One of several such atrocity stories reads: "In one house, they found two aged, helpless, unarmed men; and butchered them both without mercy, stabbing them, breaking their skulls, and dashing out their brains."

The chapter ends with a chorus of contemporary voices, chosen to affirm Bancroft's own views; in the rough draft, he had started to use the Clark quotation along with the Adams quote which closes the Lexington section, but he crossed it out so that his reflections on the day as a whole might balance Emerson of Concord with Clark of Lexington: " 'The next news from England must be conciliatory, or the connection between us ends,' said Warren. 'This month,' so William Emerson of Concord, who had been chaplain to the provincial congress, chronicled in a blank leaf of his almanac, 'is remarkable for the greatest events of the present age.' 'From the nineteenth of April, 1775,' said Clark, of Lexington, on its first anniversary, 'will be dated the liberty of the American world.' "

II *Narrative Synthesis in the Constitution Volumes*

Bancroft had early begun collecting materials on the immediate post-Revolutionary period, and the *History of the Formation of the Constitution* was the product of six years of steady labor. Younger historians already regarded Bancroft as an anachronism, but no one had yet produced so authoritative a study of the period. Bancroft was the master of his materials, and age had neither diminished his energy nor altered his style. In the words of Russel B. Nye, this work is "in many ways the finest thing that Bancroft had ever done, the most unified, thoughtful, and least partisan of his works" (Nye, p. 291).

The *Constitution* volumes are written from the same philosophic viewpoint which informs the *History*. The discipline of history remains a branch of moral philosophy: "History carries forward the study of ethics by following the footsteps of states from the earliest times of which there is a record. . . . To find moral truth, he must study man in action. The laws of which reason is conscious can be tested best by experience; and inductions will be the more sure, the larger the experience from which they are drawn" (I, 5). Both the statesman and the individual man may expect to profit from Bancroft's historical "science."

The epigraph to both volumes is W. E. Gladstone's remark that, "As the British Constitution is the most subtle organism which has proceeded from progressive society, so the American constitution is the most wonderful work ever struck off at a given time by the brain and purpose of man." Bancroft's work shows the same admiration for the Constitution and its makers, along with a serene confidence in the direction taken by "progressive history." Bancroft looked on the new age of steamships and telegraphs in which he found himself, and he found it good: "we live in the morning of the world" (I, 5). He saw in the Constitution an emblem of the progress inevitable in a history shaped by "the hand or will of a higher power" (I, 6), and he regarded the nation it brought together as "the only hope for renovating the life of the civilized world" (II, 367).

Holding such views, Bancroft shaped his *Constitution* volumes in the same pattern as his *History*—to portray the coming of union out of disunion, which is seen as the inevitable triumph of an idea. The Confederation was not so much an alternative path as a wrong turning: "In their first formative effort they missed the plain road of English and American experience" (I, 11). As usual, Bancroft advances such views as his explanation of the meaning of events; men, rather than ideas, make the events of his story. Despite rhetorical flourishes, the *Constitution* volumes present the results of original and extensive research that is rather more thoroughly documented than is sometimes the case in the *History*.

If any aspect of Bancroft's view of history may be said to have had an unfortunate effect on the *Constitution*, it would be his narrowly political view of the historical process. The Revolution was somewhat more amenable to treatment as a contest for sovereignty between peoples divided principally by democracy—though even in the *History* Bancroft's habit of speaking of a united "people" leads him to downplay the extent of Loyalist feeling and to obscure its nature. The making of the Constitution altered, and was meant to alter, the internal arrangements of power. Bancroft is happiest when the conflicts which result are between sectional or political entities—North versus South, small states versus large states. The issue, for him, is always one of yielding sovereignty to the national government; and he has little regard for the arguments and motives of those who resisted this "plain road."[5]

"The subject," said Bancroft, "has perfect unity, and falls of itself into five epochs or acts" (I, xvi). Its unity, of course, is imposed by Bancroft's view of his subject. He is not presenting the chronicle of a period but a narrative of an action—the adoption of the Federal Constitution. The basic events in this action are few in number: the

Annapolis convention of 1786, the Constitutional Convention itself, the ratification of the Constitution by the required number of states, and the actual establishment of the new government. Everything else in his narrative exists because of its relationship to these events.

Bancroft's "five epochs or acts" are dealt with in as many books: "The Confederation" (I, 3-113); "On the Way to a Federal Convention, 1783-1787" (I, 117-278); "The Federal Convention" (II, 3—222); "The People of the States in Judgment on the Constitution, 1787-1788" (II. 225-318); and "The Federal Government" (II. 321-67). One volume for events from the end of the war until the Constitution Convention, one volume for the Convention and its aftermath—this drastic fore-shortening is reminiscent of the structure of the ten-volume *History*. Unlike the *History*, this work is a complex plot in an Aristotelian sense, and the Convention is its turning point. The fortunes of the new nation decline steadily from the initial glory of the successful Revolution; by the end of the first volume, the country is in a "state of despair" because of "The utter failure of congress alike in administration and in reform, the rapid advances of the confederation toward ruin" (I, 270). The Convention is called to reverse this disintegration, and the success of its proposals is seen as assuring the future progress of the United States.

The matters dealt with in the first volume are thus almost entirely scenic in function, for no real attempt is made to present a rounded picture of even the political history of the Confederation period. What is important in the period, for Bancroft, is what looks forward to the framing of the Constitution—the failures of the Confederation and the various efforts to move toward a stronger central government. It is possible to see the Confederation as surprisingly successful in dealing with the problems of a new country under difficult conditions; but the reader does not see that in Bancroft. To see this one-sidedness as a simple failure to seek or present the "truth" would be misleading. Bancroft does not see the successes of the Confederation period as important to his action; but its problems and failures are, so he dwells on them.

Book I, "The Confederation," takes the story to the end of the war and to the dissolution of the Continental Army. The first chapter begins with "the first American union" (I, 6), a temporary union of three New England colonies against the Dutch in 1643; other efforts, successful and unsuccessful, at devising some form of union are sketched in; and there is a brief account of the wartime organization of the Confederation. Even here, Bancroft stresses that some, including Washington, felt from the first the need for a stronger government. The second chapter, "The Struggle for Revenue: 1781, 1782," treats the financial problems of the country, attributing them more to the struggles between the states and the central government than to the war. The chapter ends with a congressional commission's resolution of a boundary dispute between Connecticut and Pennsylvania, "a shining example" of "How beneficent was the authority of the union" (I, 45). The next two chapters discuss the peace negotiations and foreign affairs in 1782-83; they seem less clearly related to Bancroft's main theme, but he does bring in European doubts about the stability of the American union. The last three chapters cover Congress's problem in trying to disband an army it could not fairly pay for its service. The book closes with the "legacy of Washington," his final circular letter urging a new constitution to guarantee a strong national government.

Book II, "On the Way to a Federal Convention, 1783-1787," is mainly concerned with efforts to promote a stronger union. The titles indicate the content: Chapter I, "How the Land Received the Legacy of Washington"; Chapter III, how "Virginia Statesmen Lead Toward a Better Union." Chapter II treats "The West" as important because "The desire to hold and to people the great western domain mingled with every effort for imparting greater energy to the union" (I, 168). Chapter IV deals with the revenue problem and the regulation of commerce and concludes that "Through congress no hope for the regeneration of the union could be cherished" (I, 209). Chapter V is mostly concerned with the state of religion and with religious freedom under the Confederation; its title, "Obstacles to Union Removed or Quieted," indicates Bancroft's way of tying this material to his main theme. Chapter VI, "State Laws Impairing the Obligation of Contracts Prove the Need of an Overruling Union," shows the persistence of Bancroft's hard-money Jacksonianism in its rejection of "the evils of paper-money" (I, 240). Much of Chapter VII is devoted to George Washington, but its thesis is that Congress was finally recognizing its inability either to govern effectively or to correct its deficiencies. The last chapter deals with the Annapolis convention and its call for a new constitutional convention.

Book III, "The Federal Convention," is the longest of the work, as befits its place at the center of the action. Interpolated in its midst is a rather odd chapter, "The Colonial System of the United States," which gives the story of the Northwest Ordinance of 1787, as well as a few details on its clause barring slavery; this chapter, which simply does not fit, would seem to be an instance in which Bancroft's habit of proceeding chronologically impairs the unity of his narrative. Except for chapters on the first and last days of the convention, the rest of this book is organized topically. Three chapters treat the issue of representation; other chapters provide a general outline of the constitution and then a detailed review of its principle provisions; in each case, the relevant debates are followed to their conclusions.

Book IV, "The People of the States in Judgment on the Constitution, 1787-1788," covers a longer, more complex story in half as many pages as were devoted to the convention. Bancroft's apportioning of his space implies that the crucial act was the successful framing of this "most wonderful work." Since his previous books had argued that the "people" had come to see the need for it, their judgment is an expected one. Bancroft covers events in various state conventions, but he omits those which delayed ratification (New York, North Carolina, and Rhode Island). This omission is dictated by the general form of his action: he is not concerned with the complete political history of the period but with a single action, the formation and adoption of the Constitution. Events in the states which ratified the Constitution are a part of this action; events in states which delayed are not.

New Hampshire and Virginia, the ninth and tenth states, both ratified the Constitution on June 25, 1788; only nine were required to give it effect: "As the glad tidings flew through the land, the heart of its people thrilled with joy that at last the tree of union was firmly planted" (II, 318). If the convention is the turning point of the book's action, the climax is that the victory is won. What follows, Book V, "The Federal Government, June, 1787," is accordingly the briefest of the work's five "acts." Its function is rather like the epilogue of an old-fashioned novel in which the author, not content to have shown the lovers at last united, rounds his work off with moral reflections, ties up loose plot ends, and gives a description of their wedding ceremony. In Bancroft's work, the moral reflections take the form of an essay on the historical significance of the new constitution. The second of the three chapters in Book V ties up loose ends by reporting on New York's ratification of the Constitution and by leaving North Carolina and Rhode Island favorably disposed to the new government. The ceremony which closes the book is the inauguration of Washington.

Bancroft reinforces the unity of his action by making Washington the hero of the *Constitution* volumes, as he is of the later books of the

History. In the first book on the *Constitution*, Washington's desire for a stronger central power is mentioned early, and he naturally plays an important role in arranging the orderly disbandment of the Continental Army; Book I ends with his call for a stronger government. Book II begins with the national reaction to his call and with his triumphal progress home. Although he did not play an active role in the politics of the Confederation, in Chapter II his continued belief in the need for a stronger union is cited. Chapter III emphasizes his views on the West, Chapters V and VI mention his opinions on religious freedom and paper money, and a third of Chapter VII is devoted to a sketch of his character in temporary retirement from public life. The eighth and last chapter closes the book and volume with an account of Washington's preparations for the coming Constitutional Convention. As its presiding officer, he did not play an important role in its debates; but Book III ends with Washington dining with his fellow delegates and then retiring "at an early hour of the evening . . . 'to meditate on the momentous work which had been executed' " (II, 222). During the ratification struggle, Washington was active mainly in Virginia and was not the most active there; but his views are cited repeatedly in Book IV. His inauguration as President is thus an appropriate ending for the work.[6]

In the *History*, Washington had been a principal agent; in the *Constitution* volumes, he serves as a unifying hero more because of his wisdom than because of his acts. It might be fairer to say that the idea of a stronger union, as worked out in the Constitution, is the true protagonist of these volumes, and that Washington becomes their hero because he is seen as the man who most nearly embodies its wisdom. In 1836, Bancroft had been able to take notes during a visit with James Madison (I, ix-xi), and the energetic Madison naturally plays an important role in his account; other figures, like Jefferson and Hamilton, are also important agents in the action. But only Washington is given a fully rounded character; his presence and prescience are kept before the reader; and he emerges at the end as the living symbol of the national unity fostered by the Constitution.

The detail with which Bancroft considers the provisions of the Constitution tends to dwarf the merely human—his Washington was never that—men who debate them. If its advocates suffer by this emphasis, its opponents suffer even more so. Probably the most thoroughly treated is Richard Henry Lee of Virginia. In 1784, "Congress had put at its head the most determined and the most restlessly indefatigable opponent of any change whatever in the articles of confederation" (I, 175). The "restlessly" and "any change whatever" suggest without stating that Lee's objections were somehow almost irrational; and, indeed, Bancroft never really explores Lee's motives and arguments. The language which reports Lee's opposition to the Constitution, when proposed, is consistently loaded: Lee "claimed to discern a strong tendency to aristocracy in every part of the proposed constitution, which he slighted as the work of visionary young men" (II, 230); he "waylaid Gerry when bound for home" (II, 230); he "disingenuously" altered his arguments and "extended his intrigues" to other states (II, 230). Bancroft later reproves Patrick Henry for securing at Madison's expense the election of Lee and Grayson as Senators from Virginia (II, 354).[7]

Bancroft's volume cannot be said to give a rounded picture either of the Confederation period or of the struggle over ratification. But even in the *History* Bancroft's strength is not so much in answering the "why" of history as in a powerful description of "how" it happened. His strong convictions leave some matters outside his vision but enable him to focus clearly on what he sees. Bancroft's story has the unity he attributes to it; its parts are generally well subordinated to a clearly conceived whole, an action unified by the theme of union and by the presence of Washington. This solid narrative structure lends the *Constitution* a coherence which, with its painstaking research, still makes its power felt today.

III   *Episode and Exposition: Paper Money and the Constitution*

The *Constitution* volumes, less leisurely than the last units of the *History*, do not allow Bancroft to lavish two full chapters on the events of a single day. Even Book III must cover the four months of the convention in eleven chapters but no other period is given such detailed treatment. There is thus no set piece equivalent to the chapters on Lexington and Concord. These volumes pose, instead, another typical problem of the narrative historian—constructing a running narrative out of events treated at a rather abstract level, and Bancroft's chapter on the paper money crisis is a representative example. Moreover, much of any narrative history is actually exposition rather than narration; in Bancroft's case, this exposition often seems more like exhortation, and Book V's chapter on the Constitution is an unusually fully developed example.

Bancroft considers the issue of paper money in Chapter VI of Book

II, "State Laws Impairing the Obligation of Contracts Prove the Need of an Overruling Union: Before May, 1787." The problems of financing the war had led Congress and various states to issue paper money, just as in Bancroft's time the Civil War had led Congress to issue "greenbacks." The economic depression which started in 1784 led to demands for an increased monetary supply. In the era in which Bancroft was writing, similar conditions led to demands for free silver, but in the period about which he wrote the agitation took the form of movements for paper money, which reached a political crest in 1786. Bancroft was a hard-money Jacksonian who had been a creditor for more of his life than he had been a debtor; inevitably, he saw government-induced inflation as a threat to stability and as a dishonorable way of avoiding contractual obligations. The depression which led to the popular demand for paper money scarcely enters his pages; and when, in a later chapter, he treats Shays' Rebellion, the farmers of Massachusetts who rose to demand alleviation of their hardships are not credited with the same intuitive wisdom as those who had fought at Lexington and Concord. Only the surface reasons for their protest are recognized: "the devices of attorneys to increase their own emoluments," the "barbarous laws" permitting imprisonment for debt, and "The real cause . . . the failure of the state of Massachusetts to meet its obligations; and, still more, the bankruptcy of the general government" (I, 274-75). Governor Bowdoin is praised, therefore, for his firmness in putting down a movement which "assumed the aspect of an insurrection, almost of a rebellion" (I, 274).

The chapter dealing with the paper-money movement therefore treats it as an episode in the decline of the Confederation—another piece of evidence that a stronger central government was required. Far from suggesting that economic instability led to demands for paper money, Bancroft's chapter opens with a passage suggesting just the opposite: "A brilliant artist has painted Fortune as a beautiful woman enthroned on a globe, which for the moment is at rest, but is ready to roll at the slightest touch. A country whose people are marked by inventive genius, industry, and skill, whose eminent domain is exuberantly fertile, whose abounding products the rest of the world cannot dispense with, may hold her fast, and seat her immovably on a pedestal of four square sides. The thirteen American states had a larger experience of the baleful consequences of paper money than all the world besides" (I, 228).

Bancroft then observes that the issuance of money of varying value by the various states was not merely confusing and inconvenient but difficult for creditors, who were "liable at any time to loss by some fitful act of separate legislation" (I, 229). He next describes the wartime issuance of paper money and its peacetime discontinuation in Connecticut, Massachusetts, and New Hampshire. Connecticut, as the first to return to specie, comes in for special praise: "The widespread movements of 1786 for the issue of paper money never prevailed within its borders. Its people, as they were frugal, industrious, and honest, dwelt together in peace, while other states were rent by faction" (I, 230). The implication seems to be that those other states lacked the necessary qualities of frugality, industry, and honesty.

The next few pages review on a state-by-state basis the developments of 1786. Significantly, all of the individual men whose opinions are quoted and most of those whose views are cited are those who opposed paper money in any form. The unruly character of the movement is stressed: when checked for some time in New Jersey, "the effigy of Livingston, the aged governor, was drawn up to the stake near Elizabeth, but not consigned to the flames from reverence for the first magistrate of the commonwealth; that of a member of the council was burned" (I, 234). Had Livingston been a pre-Revolutionary governor in ill-favor with his people, Bancroft would not have remarked on his being "aged." Virginia is the last state treated, for "The redemption of the country from the blight of paper money depended largely on Virginia" (I, 237). The firm opposition of Madison and Washington is given special weight.

The chapter ends with the lesson learned—"The mind of the country bent itself with all its energy to root out the evils of paper money and establish among the states one common rule by which the obligation of contracts might be preserved unimpaired" (I, 240)—yet another example of Bancroft's identifying his view of what is morally right and historically inevitable with the "mind of the country." The interests of the propertied classes are identified with the need for reform, but Bancroft does not consider the possibility that the reforms proposed in the Constitution might have been designed to serve those classes: "For resisting reform, Rhode Island and North Carolina were likely to be the foremost; for demanding it, and for persisting in the demand, Connecticut had the most hopeful record. Among the statesmen to whom the country might look in the emergency, no one had been more conspicuous or more efficient than Madison; but Roger Sherman had all the while been a member of the supreme court of his own state, and so by near observation under great responsibility had thoroughly studied every aspect of the obligation of contracts" (I, 241). The sudden introduction of Sherman seems at first an odd note on which to end the chapter; Bancroft may be trying to tie this chapter's praise of Connecticut to his main theme; for Sherman was the man in the convention who introduced the Connecticut Compromise, whereby representation in the lower house would be proportionate to population and representation in the upper house by states.

Although accurate enough in its facts, Bancroft's is obviously not a balanced or fair account of the paper-money controversy; and his economic views are clearly both biased and in good part wrong. Yet his handling of the controversy is explainable and partially justifiable in the light of the episode's place in his action. He is concerned with those elements in the controversy which bore on the framing of the Constitution. Sad experience and sadder introspection may tell us that Bancroft is wrong to say, "Paper money has no hold, and from its very nature can acquire no hold, on the conscience or affections of the people" (II, 135), but most of those who framed the Constitution would have agreed with Bancroft. The Constitution's first article does give Congress the power to coin money, and it prohibits the states from doing so, from making anything but gold and silver legal tender, and from making any "Law impairing the Obligation of Contracts."

The conception and structure of Bancroft's chapter thus derives from that of the work as a whole. The problem—and it is also an esthetic one—is that Bancroft sees the Constitution as the product of the wisdom of a "people." The effect of this view is that he usually tells only one side of the conflicts which preceded and followed its framing; paper-money enthusiasts and anti-Federalists receive less of a hearing than did the British during and before the Revolution; for these two groups do not fit into Bancroft's picture of a united people. As a narrative history moves up the ladder of abstraction from such detailed accounts as the chapters on Lexington and Concord toward the sort of selective, general account represented by the chapter on paper money, the shaping power of the author's predispositions becomes more apparent. If Bancroft were an analytic historian, defending a thesis and overlooking negative evidence, we would have to reject his work; but Bancroft is simply trying to construct a coherent narrative, and the deficiencies of this chapter are a less serious fault. His failure to make sense of the motives of the paper money advocates is, however, a narrative fault as well as a historiographic one, for it makes the narrative as a whole that much less intelligible.

Analytic historians, after all, speak as reasoning beings participating in an abstract dialectic slowly advancing toward truth—though this idea of decorum is not always fulfilled; the narrative historian speaks as a man to men. This is, in fact, the distinguishing mark of the narrative manner of presentation: Dramas are acted out before us; lyrics are like diaries or letters, private messages somehow become public property; but the narrator always addresses us directly. When we speak of a historian's "style," we are usually speaking of the quality of his narrative voice, more than of the details of phrasing and narrative connection which we discuss in the next chapter of this study. In pursuit of some ideal of objective history or Jamesian fiction, the narrator may decline to give us his personal opinions, but he is still present in his voice; a James novel is distinctively Jamesian, and even the most academic of histories says something about its author.

Bancroft's narrative voice is a very public and solemn one. The public voice of our own time is customarily that of a lawyer at its best and that of a football coach at its worst; the kind of elevation at which Bancroft customarily aims we reserve for special occasions—inaugural addresses and elegies for assassinated heroes. When our modern historians are not trapped into the prose of politicians or the jargon of academics, they emulate the best of our novelists, some in the line of Hemingway, some in the line of James. Bancroft came of age in an era which still appreciated the oration as an art, and not only in the pulpit; he admired Sir Walter Scott, but his real affinity is with the more public rhetoric of the oration. Even Bancroft does not orate all the time; passages of action are dealt with in a style much like that of a modern historian, nineteenth-century only in a few aspects of diction and in a fondness for balanced clauses. But oratorical passages are common enough to seem a distinctive part of his narrative voice, and they form the basis for most attacks on Bancroft's style.

Bancroft's rhetorical excursions are not always very interesting, but we may note that their direct address to the reader merely makes obvious the basis of all narrative manner. We might also note that, unlike critics, readers rarely object to authorial asides. The longest such passage in Bancroft's *Constitution* volumes is Book V, Chapter I, "The Constitution."

The essay demonstrates how the Jacksonian radicalism of Bancroft's first days in politics had become, more through the passage of time than through any alteration of his views, a kind of conservatism. It begins by showing that the Constitution was a product of a tradition rather than a sharp break with the past, for its framers did not crave "untried experiments" (II, 322). It describes how various nations were assimilated by the land, so that they became one English-speaking people, whose "distinctive character . . . was the principle of individuality" (II, 325), which found expression in the Constitution most remarkably in the guarantee of freedom of religion. Bancroft acknowledges that the Constitution accommodates itself to the anomaly of slavery, but implies that its eventual extinction was inevitable since "freedom of labor was the moral principle of the majority of the people" (II, 326). Reviewing the structure of the government, he singles out the separation of powers (legislative, executive, and judicial), the difficulty of making amendments, and the reservation of many powers in the hands of the states; and each of these is seen as a protection against reckless change and despotism.

The chapter ends with a glance at the future of the republic and at its possible effect on other nations and with a final passage that once more identifies Bancroft's own views with those of the people: "The philosophy of the people of the United States was neither that of optimism nor of despair. Believing in the justice of 'the great Governor of the world,' and conscious of their own honest zeal in the cause of freedom and mankind, they looked with astonishment at their present success and at the future with unclouded hope" (II, 335). While the content of the chapter is Bancroft's summary of the meaning of his story as he sees it, a meaning that reflects his views on contemporary issues as well, its shape is thus roughly chronological: we begin with distinguished forerunners; we proceed to the formation of a distinctive people; the leading characteristics of the Constitution are set forth; and we conclude with a glance at the future. Bancroft's meditations on his subject follow the pattern of its action, and of the *History*, to which he was soon to append these volumes.

CHAPTER *5*

The Road to "The Author's Last Revision"

T HE careful workmanship that marked Bancroft's drafting of the Lexington and Concord chapters was not the end of his passion for revising. He made some minor revisions in successive revisions of his individual volumes; and, after the 1874 appearance of Volume X of the *History*, he set to work on a more extensive revision of the whole work, which appeared in 1875-76 as the six-volume Centenary Edition. After he had completed the *Constitution* volumes, he decided to incorporate them with the *History* in yet another revision. This work took him three years to complete; and, although he continued to speak of bringing his history down to the Jacksonian period, his subtitle makes a melancholy acknowledgment of his advanced age and the likelihood that this would be "The Author's Last Revision."[1]

Bancroft's preface sets for this revision the same goals as for the original work—accuracy unclouded by mere speculation and "lucidity in the ordering of the narrative" (ALR, I, iv). The preface also reflects his concerns with criticisms made of his ornate style and shows that Bancroft had labored to accommodate himself to the tastes of a new age: "Repetitions and redundancies have been removed; greater precision has been sought for; the fitter word that offered itself accepted; and, without the surrender of the right of history to pronounce its opinion, care has been taken never unduly to forestall the judgment of the reader, but to leave events as they sweep onward to speak their own condemnation or praise" (ALR, I, v). Even as revised, Bancroft's volumes do not display in practice quite so much concern for the reader's independence of judgment. Comparison of the original volumes with their final form may help point to the general characteristics of Bancroft's method, as well as display its evolution over a long period of time. It might be thought (and is sometimes asserted) that the earliest volumes were the most heavily revised, but this view is incorrect; nevertheless, we shall begin with Volume I. The same processes are also at work in the other volumes, thereby giving the revised work stylistic unity. Since the revision is Bancroft's final statement, it may enable us to offer some observations on historical explanation in the *History*.

I   *Volume I of the* History, *1834-1885*

The content of Volume I of the *History* takes up only the first half of the first volume of "The Author's Last Revision," but most of the 147-page difference can be accounted for by the use of smaller print. In matters of substance, more is added than is lost. A few incidents have been moved from place to place within the volume, but most of the revision simply carries forward the movement toward a more condensed narrative. Some of these stylistic revisions affect the tone of the work, but most contribute only brevity.

A careful examination shows almost no incidents of any conceivable importance omitted in the revision. One of the longest single omissions eliminates almost a page of material beginning with the second sentence of the original volume (I, 5-6) and concerning itself with the arguments for the Northmen's discovery and colonization of North America before Columbus. More persuasive arguments have since appeared—the Vinland map—but the matter is still by no means clear. Bancroft surveyed the evidence available to him, found it vague and unreliable, and concluded that, while such "intrepid mariners" were certainly capable of reaching Labrador from Greenland, "no clear historic evidence establishes the natural probability that they accomplished the passage" (I, 6). The Northmen have disappeared from the revision except for the retention of a later speculation that "some uncertain traditions respecting the remote discoveries which Icelanders had made in Greenland toward the north-west" (I, 8; ALR, I, 9) may have influenced the English in sending John Cabot to look for new lands and for a northwest passage to Asia.

The omission of the Icelandic speculations has the effect of focusing attention on Columbus in the first few pages, and the same goal is served by Bancroft's additions. The revised version refers to earlier arguments that the earth was a sphere, a more relevant topic than the Northmen's explorations since it bears on the cosmographic and cartographic tradition which actually influenced Columbus. Another addition to the account of Columbus shows that Bancroft had indeed not surrendered "the right of history to pronounce its opinion": " 'Lord, into thy hands I commend my spirit,' were the words of

Columbus, as on Ascension Day, 1506, he breathed his last. His great discovery was the triumph of free mind. In the year of his death, Copernicus, like him, emancipated from authority, attained the knowledge of the true theory of our solar system" (ALR, I, 13).

The minor changes made in the last three paragraphs of the chapter are mainly aimed at eliminating superfluous words and at making the account more specific. The original reads: "in the summer, when the Pilgrims were leaving Leyden, in obedience to the wishes of the unhappy Montmorenci, the new viceroy, Champlain, began a fort" (I, 29). The Pilgrims are unnecessary, the syntax ambiguous, and the "unhappy" pejorative. The revision reads: "in July, 1620, in obedience to the wishes of Montmorenci, the new viceroy, Champlain, began a fort" (ALR, I, 21). In other revisions (on the same pages), "in a few years" has become "in 1624"; we are told that Richelieu "had been created Grand Master of Navigation"; and an oratorical "Thus" has been removed from the beginning of the chapter's last sentence. These and other changes in the first chapter make it no longer but more lucid in outline and more specific in detail; and these revisions set the pattern for the revisions in the volume as a whole.

The second chapter of Volume I, "Spaniards in the United States," has become three chapters in the revision. In part, this change reflects a desire for shorter chapters; the ten of the original volume have become nineteen in "The Author's Last Revision." But Bancroft has also added some new material, particularly about Spanish explorations west of the Mississippi River. These additions are partly balanced by a reduction of Bancroft's generalizations about the Spanish character. The chapter on Virginia, which becomes two chapters in the revision, has also been expanded—new material on efforts to plant a second colony there, a paragraph on the Spanish reaction to the English presence, and more material on the colony in 1620-21, especially on the role of Sir Edwin Sandys. These additions redress in part the first volume's initial over-concentration on Bancroft's own New England. There are no other major additions to the volume.

In general, the outline of incidents in the revision follows that of the original almost exactly. Bancroft's account of the marriage of Pocahontas and John Rolfe is now placed after an English attack on a French settlement in Maine and a Shakespearean salute to James as the founder of colonies. In this change, we see a return to a stricter chronological order. Some comments on John Smith's voyage to New

England and later career have been moved from a chapter on the Pilgrims to the end of the first chapter on the colonization of Virginia, and the reader is enabled to follow all of Smith's adventures in one chapter. Like the added details about Columbus, Sebastian Cabot, and Sir Edwin Sandys, this addition contributes to the slightly more prominent role of individual men in the revision.

A very few changes present different interpretations of events. One of these concerns John Smith's alleged rescue from death at the hands of Powhatan by the intervention of Pocahontas, the chieftain's ten- or twelve-year-old daughter. Bancroft originally accepted Smith's account of this episode:

The gentle feelings of humanity are the same in every race, and in every period of life; they bloom, though unconsciously, even in the bosom of a child. Smith had easily won the confiding fondness of the Indian maiden; and now the impulse of mercy awakened within her breast; she clung firmly to his neck, as his head was bowed to receive the strokes of the tomahawk. Did the child-like superstition of her kindred reverence her interference as a token from a superior power? Her fearlessness and her entreaties persuaded the council to spare the agreeable stranger, who might make hatchets for her father, and rattles and strings of beads for herself, the favorite child. (I, 131)

This mixture of legend and speculation has disappeared in the revision, along with some other material from Smith's account of his captivity. All that remains is a skeptical reference to Pocahontas as "The child, to whom in later days he attributed his rescue" (ALR, I, 93). Bancroft was willing to sacrifice a good story that did not meet his standards of truth.

A rather more serious change is Bancroft's interpretation of Bacon, a change indicated by one in the tables of content from "Lord Bacon's Tolerant Views" (I, xi) to "Intolerance of Bacon" (ALR, I, xi). The tolerant Bacon of the first volume receives high marks from his historian for his "profound philosophy" and "vigorous mind" (I, 294). A less glowing tribute is paid to the intolerant Bacon of the revision: "The great master of speculative wisdom knew too little of religion to inculcate freedom of conscience" (ALR, I, 202). His failure to do so, despite his recognition of the faults of the established church, is attributed to weakness of character: "But Bacon was formed for contemplative life, not for action; his will was feeble, and yet, having an incessant yearning for vain distinction and display, he became a craven courtier and an intolerant statesman" (ALR, I, 203). A minor hero has become a minor villain.

The attitudes toward history sketched in Chapter I of this study clung to all of Bancroft's life. Moreover, they were embedded in the very structure of his first volume. The revision retains the structure and with it the tendency to see all issues as political ones and to judge the importance of past events by their relevance to the future. History remains the story of an inevitable progress guided by a providential Power. But the revision does spend somewhat less time instructing the reader in this way of viewing history; bent on reducing his narrative, Bancroft retained all major incidents but sacrificed some of his rhetoric.

What this revision meant in practice may be seen by a comparison of the closing pages of Part I of the revision (Chapter XIX, "The Place of Puritanism in History"; ALR, I, 311-22) with the final pages of the original (I, 446-69). Bancroft is particularly concerned in these pages with the intolerance shown by the Puritans to other sects. In the original, he alternates between explaining why the Puritans were wrong to be intolerant and why it was natural for them to be so. Both the denunciatory and extenuating rhetoric have been cut a good bit, though almost no single incident from the original has been omitted.

The first major cut is a page-long paragraph arguing that "Where the mind is left free, religion can have no dangerous enemies" (I, 447-48). Bancroft is now willing to trust his readers to reject bigotry and governmental restraints upon religious practice. The next paragraph, which explains that, after all, "the freemen of the New World" were eventually to undergo an "emancipation from bigotry" (I, 448)—another plea for the reader's patience with the Puritans—has also been eliminated. On the next page, Bancroft eliminates a few sentences claiming that "the people did not entirely respond to these extravagant views" (I, 449), sentences that simply reflect Bancroft's desire to show the "people" as always wiser than their leaders. These cuts—and small type—crowd three pages of the original into one.

The Quakers suffered most of all from the Puritans of Massachusetts, for they would not stay banished, and for a time the Puritans were prepared to hang even women who were especially obstinate about returning. Bancroft admires the Quakers' courage, deplores their intransigence, and is outraged by the punishments inflicted upon them. In the original volume he is careful to point out that "the Quakers in New England displayed little of the mild philosophy, the statesman-like benevolence, of Penn and his disciples," but he soon redresses the balance by writing of the sect as a consequence of "the aspiration of the human mind after a perfect emancipation from the long reign of bigotry and superstition" (I, 451). Both observations are deleted in the revision. In the original, the death penalty is described as an "atrocity" and a "crime" (I, 454); these descriptions, and the paragraphs which supported them, are gone. There are similar excisions of other passages denouncing religious bigotry, speaking of the eccentricities and deficiencies of some of the Quakers, and arguing that "It was in self-defense that Puritanism in America began those transient persecutions of which the excesses shall find in me no apologist" (I, 463).

Despite these cuts, Bancroft's attitudes remain in the revision; only the rhetoric which embodied them has been considerably reduced, so that the events speak more for themselves. He clearly regrets the Puritans' intolerance and is disposed to see it as a passing thing— "Massachusetts was in the state of transition when expiring bigotry exhibited its worst aspect" (ALR, I, 311). We are still told that "The people were averse to taking Quakers' lives" (ALR, I, 315), and the Quakers are still "half fanatic, half insane" (ALR, I, 312), and thus partially responsible for the excesses to which their persecutors were led. And the chapter still ends with the inclusion of a long paragraph comparing the Puritan spirit favorably to the chivalric one.

Not all of the rhetoric eliminated in the revision was interpretative; Bancroft also excised a number of largely decorative flights of fancy. The original reads that "the doctrine of toleration, with the pledges of peace, hovered like the dove at the window of the ark, waiting to be received into its rightful refuge" (I, 458). The dove is gone in the revision: "the doctrine of toleration, with pledges of peace, was soon to be received" (ALR, I, 315). An example of an even more purely stylistic change is the reduction of "any man's person to be kept in prison for debt" (I, 466) to "any imprisonment for debt" (ALR, I, 321). Such small changes contribute as much to the lesser bulk of the revision as do the less frequent major excisions. The narrative structure remains intact and perhaps can be seen more clearly in the more straightforward prose of the revision.

II   *"The Author's Last Revision"*

The pattern set by the first volume's revision is that of the whole. Of the two remaining volumes of the history of the colonization, Volume III has received the more extensive revision. Most of Bancroft's important changes in these two volumes add material about the efforts of various European powers to populate and control the new continent. Volume II has some added material about the Dutch and New Netherlands and a few added paragraphs on the English debate over the abrogation of the charter of Massachusetts. Volume III introduces added material on the French in America and on developments in both France and England. The amount of additional material looks greater than it is, for Bancroft has also rearranged the contents of this volume more than in any other. The original volume opens with one long chapter which ties together developments in England and America after the Glorious Revolution of 1688. Volume II of "The Author's Last Revision" opens with separate chapters on developments in the Southern, Middle, and New England colonies, followed by an expanded account of "Parliament and the Colonies." The original volume then takes up the French settlements and some early struggles among the great powers for control of the West, continuing this story only after a chapter on the Amerindians; but the revision's three chapters on the Indians precede any detailed account of the struggle over their territory. The added material reflects the assimilation of Bancroft's researches in Europe, and others' efforts as well (notably Parkman's); but the rearrangement seems dictated by an even stronger conception of the events covered as part of a European power struggle.

Few of Bancroft's changes in these volumes reflect any fundamental changes in his attitudes toward history or his interpretation of particular events. If he retains his faith in the efficacy of impartial research—"facts, faithfully ascertained and placed in proper contiguity, become of themselves the firm links of a brightly burnished chain, connecting events with their causes" (ALR, II, 269, following III, 398)—he still follows this passage with declarations of his belief in the rule of moral law, the reality of progress, and the workings of Divine Providence. Some limited evidence exists of an occasional attempt to allow the reader to form his own opinion of men and events. The original contains a long paragraph of unflattering comment and speculation about the character of Cotton Mather and his behavior during the Salem witch trials: "Was Cotton Mather honestly credulous? Ever ready to dupe himself, he limited his credulity only by the probable credulity of others" (III, 97). Although this statement is rather enjoyable reading, it does not meet even Bancroft's standards of impartial inquiry; it is gone in the revision, though Mather does not emerge with much credit from Bancroft's account.

The remainder of the revision's second volume contains the material originally included in the fourth volume of the *History*. Since Volume IV was written after Bancroft's return from Europe, there is much less new material in this section; indeed, a good bit of Bancroft's revision was evidently aimed at excising material on the European background which he had included in his first enthusiasm for the notes he had taken. The chapters are the same, too, for it was with Volume IV that Bancroft had first adopted the shorter chapter length characteristic of "The Author's Last Revision." The only exception is that the last two chapters of the original, both dealing with English and European developments, have become one short chapter in the revision. The effect of the changes made in this volume and in the first three is to produce a more even apportioning of space between American and European events.

The longest excision is the first two pages of Chapter XVIII, "The Acts of Trade Provoke Revolution." The material omitted deals with English politics; the chapter as revised confines itself to American developments. Narrative unity is also served by the omission of a paragraph mentioning an irregular colony established on the banks of the Santilla by some adventurers (IV, 242). No new incidents are added, but some new opinions are cited from contemporaries. Lord Chesterfield foresees a time of revolution (ALR, II, 376); Edmund Burke regrets the inhumane treatment of the Acadians (ALR, II, 434); and William Smith, "the semi-republican historian of New York" (ALR, II, 449), urges an American union with an American parliament. These additions come at the end of chapters and reflect either the convenience of revising chapter endings or Bancroft's continued search for effective "curtain lines."

The whole of the third volume of the revision is concerned with the second epoch of Bancroft's drama of the revolution, "Britain Estranges America"—volumes V and VI of the *History*; and the weight of Bancroft's editorial labors again falls on the European material. Volume V began with two chapters on Europe and France in 1763; the revision omits these completely and begins with a chapter on England in 1763. The omission here is of pure "scenic" material which has no important bearing on the narrative action of the volume. Although few incidents are completely cut, the maneuverings in the British parliament are given much less space in the revision. Other items omitted include a sketch of Governor Tryon of North Carolina, originally inserted at the end of a chapter dealing wholly with events in England (VI, 85-87), and some details of the actions of various colonies in 1769 concerning the non-importation agreements (VI, 316-18).

Some of the shorter chapters of the original volumes have been combined, and there is a certain amount of rearrangement. The Wilkes affair, originally treated in two widely separated chapters, is now confined to one. The first American reactions to the Stamp Act now directly follow the account of its passage; this arrangement also permits a more consolidated treatment of its immediate aftermath in British parliamentary politics. The internal arrangement of a few chapters has also been slightly altered—for example, the reactions of the various colonies to the plan for the Stamp Act before its passage. Most of these alterations are directed at permitting a more condensed narrative of events. The only notable expansion is in the revised Chapter XXXI, in which Bancroft gives more details about the opposition of important Virginians to slavery and the slave trade; no new incidents are added, but Bancroft gives fuller quotations. He cannot be said to have suppressed this material in the original, and there is no clear reason why he now expands it; perhaps the Civil War had sharpened his opinions on the subject.

The fourth and fifth volumes of the revision replace the last four volumes of the *History*. Although these were more recently from Bancroft's pen, he found much in them to omit and much he wished to rearrange, and he dealt with them rather more vigorously than he had with Volume I. As in the revision of Volumes IV through VI, he eliminated or sharply condensed a good deal of the materials he had brought back with him from Europe. The most important cut is in the last of his volumes; newly returned from diplomatic duties in Germany, Bancroft had devoted the second and third chapters of Volume X to Prussia under Frederick the Great—these chapters and most of their contents have disappeared completely in the revision. Chapters VI and VIII of the same volume have been joined together to connect the plans of Spain with the events in the American West which partly frustrated them. Chapter XX of that volume has been moved back to follow materials originally dealt with in Chapters IX through XII; the effect is to group together the chapters dealing with the British treatment of would-be neutral powers. A good portion of the structure of Volume VIII has been rearranged. The original tends to follow foreign and American events simultaneously. The revision makes it clear that once the issue is joined, Bancroft regards the American developments as the main line of action. Events abroad are either grouped in separate chapters covering longer periods of time or introduced as they become relevant to events in America.

Along with this rearrangement, Bancroft tightened his narrative, reducing anecdotal paragraphs to sentences and long quotations to a few phrases. Aside from the chapters on Prussia, few incidents are actually eliminated completely. From its original volumes, Volume IV of "The Author's Last Revision" eliminates most of a long section on France in 1774 (VII, 25-34); an account of the first public speech of Alexander Hamilton (VII, 79-80); remarks on the sad state of the French navy (VII, 93); some details of events in the South in 1775 (VIII, Chapters XLV and XLVI); a discussion of the meaning of historical impartiality and why this is easier for Americans to achieve (VIII, 116-22); Franklin's encouragement of Tom Paine and the 1775 opinions of John Adams and Tory Dr. John Zubly (VIII, 140-41); remarks on Louis XVI and the French cabinet (VIII, 329-30); and some even less important material. The fifth volume of the revision eliminates some unfavorable comments about previous historians (IX, 122-24); an argument that Washington's desire for a standing army was not motivated by any lack of faith in the common man (IX, 138); some details of Spanish history (IX, 301-303); a good bit of a survey of Europe in 1778 (X, 45-60); most of an account of the 1779 diplomacy of Frederick (X, 240-45); and an anecdote about French-speaking troops from the two armies embracing after the capture of Yorktown (X, 523). Most of these omissions contribute to the revision's down-playing of European developments; all of them are of tangential relevance to the narrative action.

Of the few additions to these volumes, none is of great importance. Two concern military action—the first formation of local regiments in Massachusetts (ALR, IV, 60) and the capture of Natchez (ALR, V, 315). Two others give us word of developments in additional states: we are told of North Carolina's support for Massachusetts in 1774 (ALR, IV, 36) and of some developments of 1775 in Vermont and Delaware (ALR, IV, 142-43).[2] The other principal additions are about characters. The unsuccessful Schuyler is now given credit for the grace with which he took being relieved from command (ALR, V, 173). Virginia's vote of thanks to George Rogers Clark is recorded (ALR, V, 316). And there is always more for Bancroft to say about Washington; in the revision, we hear of a French minister's high opinion of him (ALR, V, 319-20) and of his refusal to consider being made king (ALR, V, 558).

Volume X of the *History* ends with the colonies' lack of a strong government but possessing a "people . . . superior to its institutions" (X, 593); in the revision, their being one people gives "the sure promise of a more perfect constitution" (ALR, V, 581). The sixth volume of the revision, which shows how they devised this constitution, reprints the text of the *Constitution* volumes, shorn of their appendices of letters and documents, but with little change—perhaps one or two more accurately transcribed quotations and an occasional stylistic change. One of these does display a less effusive rhetoric at work: the original ends as "all the friends of mankind invoked success on their endeavor as the only hope for renovating the life of the civilized world" (II, 367). The revision reduces this statement to "on the unexampled endeavor to govern states and territories of imperial extent as one federal republic" (ALR, VI, 474).

It would obviously be impractical (and tedious for writer and reader alike) to account for any large portion of the more purely stylistic revisions made by Bancroft in these later volumes. To give some idea of their character, we may turn again to the Lexington and Concord chapters from Volume VII. In the revision, these have become a single chapter, "To Lexington and Concord, and Back to Boston, April 19, 1775" (ALR, IV, Chapter X). This change means no more than a lack of a chapter division between the last paragraph of the Lexington chapter and the first paragraph of the Concord chapter. The actual alterations are slight, only five representing full sentences: The opening sentence is new: "Gage, who had under his command about three thousand effective men, was informed by his spies of military stores, pitiful in their amount, collected by provincial committees at Worchester and Concord; and he resolved on striking a blow, as the king desired" (ALR, IV, 152). This opening ties together the events of the new chapter and includes material struck out in earlier drafts (cf. pp. 61-68 above). The third paragraph omits three and a half sentences which attribute Gage's order that no civilians leave the town to a remark overheard by Lord Percy (VII, 289). And at the end of the chapter Bancroft omits a sentence speculating that, if the retreat had been delayed another half-hour or had been intercepted in front by the Salem and Marblehead regiment (then just arriving), the British force might have been compelled to surrender (VII, 309; cf. ALR, IV, 165). Two other omitted sentences are purely rhetorical reflections on the minute men at Concord and the American Revolution.[3]

The remaining changes are all omissions and condensations; Bancroft shortens a sentence here and combines two others in another place, reducing the bulk of the chapter as a whole by perhaps a couple of paragraphs. A handful of these cuts have some minor effect on the tone of the chapter: the British Lieutenant-Colonel Smith is no longer directly labeled "incompetent" (VII, 288); the Lexington minute men no longer stand "as yet unsuspicious of immediate danger" (VII, 292-93); the British firing upon them is no longer "murder" as opposed to "battle" (VII, 293); and the martyred Jonas Parker of Lexington no longer possesses "as sound a heart as ever throbbed for freedom" (VII, 293). Most of what is omitted is irrelevant detail of neither narrative nor thematic importance—like the information that James Hayward of Acton was the son of its deacon (VII, 306).

Russel B. Nye has characterized the revision as showing "significant changes in approach as well as style," including a less pervasive nationalism, less blame assigned the British for the slave trade, and "appreciably fewer references to the intervention of divine Providence in American affairs" (Nye, p. 297). Our careful examination of the differences between the original volumes and the "Last Revision" indicates that the changes do not represent any new approach. The elimination of much European material makes these volumes more America centered than their predecessors, and the Americans are still the salt of the earth. Bancroft still repeatedly stresses colonial opposition to the slave trade and has even expanded one of these passages. In the interests of conciseness, some redundant passages on the meaning of history have been sacrificed; but Providence, which never directly "intervened" in his narrative, is still present as a teleological force. God has still selected Washington as a man of destiny (ALR, II, 313), and the dead of Lexington still cry for vengeance from the ground (ALR, IV, 156). Most important of all, the revision does not touch the basic narrative structure—the true embodiment of Bancroft's view of man and history.

We must qualify this generalization by observing that the addition of the *Constitution* volumes in the revision inevitably has some effect on the form of the work as a whole. The theme of union, so prominent in the early volumes, is now seen as not simply the precondition for the successful achievement of independence but as the governing theme of the work as a whole. We return, in fact, to the doctrines of Bancroft's "On Self-Government": to achieve self-government is to achieve both freedom and union. Nevertheless, the Revolution remains the climax of the book's action, for the Constitution is treated as an inevitable refinement of the union formed under the stress of war. To return to our analogy of the happy lovers and their wedding, the framing and adoption of the Constitution serve in the context provided by the revision this happy but anticlimatic function. The decline of the Confederation does not assume the importance of a true reversal, given the apportionment of space in the six volumes; and the plot remains the simple, even inevitable, rise to self-government.

III   *Narrative Sentences and the Science of History*

Bancroft's "science" of history was still a branch of moral philosophy; the younger historians to whom he spoke at the 1886 meeting of the American Historical Association were more apt to model their science on geology and paleontology and to find the evolutionary ancestors of American democracy in Germanic and Saxon institutions. Although Bancroft's style lacked the "objectivity" his younger colleagues had come to value, they had few real objections to the narrative form of his work and several were involved with projects at least as ambitious as the *History*. Henry Adams, for example, devoted nine volumes to the history of the United States in the administrations of Thomas Jefferson and James Madison (published 1889-91). Yet, as readers of *The Education of Henry Adams* (1918) will recall, Adams was also impressed with the models offered by physics and mathematics. When modern historians debate, as they sometimes do, whether history is an art or a social science, they usually follow the later Adams in taking the mathematical rigor of physics as their model of a science and in assuming that the historian's task is to develop generalizations on the model of physical laws.[4]

Although Bancroft sometimes speaks of the "laws" of history, he does not arrive at them by empirical investigation or state them with mathematical rigor. It seems very unlikely that Bancroft's narrative form, unified by a plot composed of interdependent lines of action, could serve as an appropriate vehicle for the demonstration of empirically derived generalizations about history. But historians continue to construct such narratives, and some philosophers have recently concerned themselves with the relationship between historical narratives and the kind of general laws arrived at in the natural sciences. Although narrative histories may not lead to new scientific laws about history, they may still be thought of as explaining the particular events with which they deal by accounting for them as instances of such general laws. Philosophers holding this view believe that scientific explanations are the only explanations worthy of the name; historical explanations must, therefore, follow this model.[5]

If all explanations must show that particular events are logical outcomes of general laws, it may be thought that narratives like Bancroft's do not explain anything. Since this is tantamount to saying that history as a branch of knowledge does not meet the high standard set by the natural sciences, historians have been loath to accept this conclusion, and some philosophers have attempted to find more satisfactory answers. One answer is to maintain that the lines of action in a historical narrative compose a causal chain, in which the successive incidents are related by cause and effect.[6] Our acceptance of these causal relationships would depend, in turn, on our recognition of certain regularities in human experience, regularities which might serve as the historical equivalent of the general laws found in the natural sciences.

When we turn to Bancroft's narrative, however, we find very few direct assertions of cause-and-effect relationships. For example, the chapter on the events at Lexington and Concord, as we have seen, begins with this sentence: "Gage, who had under his command about three thousand effective men, was informed by his spies of military stores, pitiful in their amount, collected by provincial committees at Worchester and Concord, and he resolved on striking a blow, as the king desired" (ALR, IV, 152). In this sentence, only the "and" and "as" suggest causality, although the sentence is in some sense an explanatory statement about the British expedition against the stores at Concord. We are given enough facts to render Gage's action plausible: he had sufficient troops; he had a military objective; and he knew that his sovereign wanted him to take firm action. But we are not presented with a full account of the relevant facts, much less with an explicit appeal to some historical generalization.

It is not difficult for us to think of suitable generalizations. We might say that the plausibility of this account depended on our acceptance of two generalizations: (1) generals will try to capture or destroy the military supplies of possible enemies, and (2) generals will try to carry out their sovereign's wishes.[7] But these are our generalizations, and we have no way of knowing whether they are Bancroft's or whether they are important to other readers. Bancroft's sentence gives us good grounds for assuming that he thought its facts related, and we are probably justified in saying that the presence of the military stores in Worchester and Concord contributes to the probability of Gage's decision to send out an expedition; but the narrative does not tell us on what basis Bancroft thought their presence made Gage's action more probable.

Very similar problems arise when we try to relate Bancroft's practice to another theory about historical explanation, that the historian proceeds by "re-thinking the past," giving us the reasons for a character's actions rather than the causes. This theory was devised by philosophers who wished to stress the special, intuitive nature of historical knowledge, making it equal to but different from the natural sciences; the distinction it makes between the reasons governing the actions of human beings and the impersonal causes governing the natural world has been rejected by many.[8] In any case, when we look at the Bancroft sentence just quoted, we do not find any reference to the reasoning which led Gage to resolve "on striking a blow." We only have a few facts about the situation in which he found himself and the bare fact of his resolve.

Once again, it would not be too difficult for us to supply the necessary rationale. We might say that the plausibility of Bancroft's account results from our being able to imagine Gage, pressed by his king to take action, learning that hostile forces were stock-piling supplies and deciding to take action. But this account of Gage's reasoning is not part of Bancroft's own narrative. Nor are we justified in saying that Bancroft's narrative implies the existence of a particular chain of reasoning. Bancroft tells us that the stores were "pitiful in their amount"—did Gage mistakenly think of them as a serious military threat or did he intend the expedition primarily as a show of force? If we were seriously engaged in re-thinking Gage's rationale for action, we would need an answer to that question, but Bancroft's narrative does not permit us to answer it with any confidence.

Before asserting that the statements in a narrative plot necessarily imply certain generalizations, we should, then, remember how cleverly and futilely literary critics have labored to prove that Shakespeare's plays are Catholic, Protestant, pro-Tudor, anti-Tudor, and vegetarian.[9] Before asserting that incidents in a narrative plot necessarily imply a set of reasons for its characters, we should call to mind the many contradictory accounts of the inner life of Hamlet. Bancroft's *History* is cast in a literary form and is subject to the fatal ambiguity of language, which has caused a good deal of trouble for philosophers themselves. To insist that historical explanations must imply certain generalizations or rationales because all explanations of human actions have such generalizations or rationales is a tautological argument; the most we can say is that Bancroft's *History* is not inconsistent with either form of explanation.

It may be objected that the Bancroft sentence quoted earlier does not raise the larger questions of causation with which historians must deal. The answer is that the bulk of Bancroft's narrative, as of most narrative histories, consists of just such sentences. For contrast, we may look at a later passage in the same chapter: speaking of the men of Lexington, Bancroft says, "They fulfilled their duty not from an accidental impulse of the moment; their action was the ripened fruit of Providence and of time" (ALR, IV, 156-57). The next sentence expands on this thought by giving an interminable catalog of fighters for freedom from the Hebrews through the Glorious Revolution. It is significant that this passage comes after his account of the Lexington skirmish; although Bancroft here appeals to a general principle, the inevitable triumph of man's desire for freedom, this passage is primarily concerned with reflection on the meaning of the event, rather than with an account of its causes. Bancroft does not argue that his heroes were directly motivated by a knowledge of Saxon customs or Luther's courage. At most, we might say that the passage contributes to the probability of the events narrated by showing that they are in tune with the previous behavior of men in history; this is still a "scenic" function, and the passage is not a part of any line of action.

It is perfectly possible to reject Bancroft's belief in man's inevitable progress toward freedom and self-government while accepting as trustworthy and worthwhile his account of the events at Lexington. Bancroft's beliefs helped him decide what story he had to tell, what form he should give it, and what its essential incidents were. If we reject Bancroft's beliefs, we may prefer a different story about the same period of history, but we are not bound to reject the connections he establishes between the events he regards as essential. We may even find a different meaning in the story than Bancroft sees; the implicit generalizations intended by the author are as suspect as any other—in literary criticism, thinking otherwise is known as the "intentional fallacy." By the same token, we might agree with Bancroft's ideas but feel he had not produced a plausible set of lines of action: in that case, we would say that his story had meaning but that he had not succeeded in linking together events. We can also imagine a careful account of, say, the cause and effect relationship between two billiard balls bouncing against each other on a table; if the story contained no reference to either a shooter or a score, it would strike most readers as meaningless, a line of action leading from nowhere to no-place. Shaggy-dog stories are jokes with no essential incidents.

It might seem that we have retreated to the point of saying that Bancroft spent fifty years of work explaining nothing, for we have argued that his narrative statements do not necessarily imply the existence of historical generalizations, of developed rationales for individual characters, or even his own deepest beliefs. This conclusion would follow only from an unduly restrictive use of the word "explanation." When we ask "Why did this happen?" we often expect the answer to take the form of a story. What we expect, then, is what Bancroft professes to give us: "facts, faithfully ascertained and placed in proper 'contiguity' " (ALR, II, 269).[10] It does not seem unreasonable, therefore, to regard narrative as an acceptable form of explanation. Nor does it seem necessary to claim the mantle of science for Bancroft's work. He does not offer us the behavioral laws some historians now search for, and we are unable to accept as scientific the moral laws Bancroft thought he had found. The younger historians he addressed in 1886 were no doubt right to regard his work as less scientific than their own; but because Bancroft was a master storyteller, the *History* has outlasted most of the work of his younger colleagues.

CHAPTER 6

The Ends of History

THE Bancroft who published "The Author's Last Revision" and spoke the next year to the American Historical Association was still a vigorous man, full of plans for new works. But, though his friends might assure him that he seemed "as youthful as ever," Bancroft knew that age was against him: "I am no longer making collections of books; but rather looking about me to see how I shall dispose of what I have, knowing that at my great age I am liable to be called away from the world at any time."[1] If he was not collecting more books, he was at any rate collecting materials for a possible book on James K. Polk. And, as his end drew near, he could look back with satisfaction upon a later career which had in good part fulfilled the promise of his youth and the ambitions which had troubled him at Round Hill. Although he was never again the powerful political figure that he was before he sailed for England, he had had a distinguished career as a diplomat; and his advice was still listened to, if not much followed, in national affairs. His career as a historian had brought him riches, fame, and friendships that he valued highly.

Bancroft never wrote his book on Polk; his last book, a biography of Martin Van Buren, was an out-of-date campaign biography. Of more interest because of what it tells us about Bancroft than for what it tells us of Van Buren, this biography adds nothing to Bancroft's stature; but the book is the principal example in Bancroft's canon of what we may call the "rhetoric" of history when we use the term to refer to the use of history to persuade a particular audience. If we evaluate Bancroft's best work, which is aimed at the general reader of any time and serves no partisan ends, we must grope for a "poetics" of history, asking ourselves why a historical narrative like Bancroft's still gives pleasure.

I *Diplomat and Elder Statesman*

Bancroft brought to diplomacy the same attitudes and abilities he brought to history. His intelligence and industry made him the master of the technical side of his duties; his European education and command of languages enabled him to move with ease in any society; and his historical knowledge gave him a ready stock of precedents to urge in negotiations and arguments. He arrived in Europe with a distrust of aristocrats in general and of English ones in particular. His greatest fault as a diplomat, one observable in the *History* as well, was a tendency to see unfolding events as confirmations of his views of history and society.

Bancroft's chief responsibilities as a Minister were, first, to report the views of the British public and its government and, second, to discourage that government from any interference with the American efforts in Mexico. The second task was not difficult so long as the superiority of American arms made the war's eventual outcome clear. He was able to negotiate a treaty regulating postal rates between the two countries, but a long effort to arrive at commercial agreements failed when the Whigs won the American election in 1848. Bancroft held to his post in hopes of concluding the agreements before resigning, but in March, 1849, the new administration told him to abandon the negotiations just as he felt that he was on the verge of success. In May, he was told that his replacement would arrive in October. Annoyed at having the change made public before he was told (and given a chance to resign with honor), he sailed home in August rather than stay to give his successor the usual welcome.

During this time, Bancroft also made a couple of visits to Paris. The American Minister there knew nothing of French, and Bancroft's reporting was useful. His dislike of monarchic regimes made him especially sensitive to signs of growing discontent. He saw the Revolution of 1848 as inspired by American democracy, and he urged American support of the liberal movements in Europe. Though always less sympathetic to the French than to the Germans, the revolution made him think the French a "wonderful people": "If these people do not get good government it will be the fault of their representatives, not of them."[2] But, despite personal friendships with some French leaders, he worried that lack of political experience meant that France was not yet ready for a republic.

Bancroft's wife reported that it first seemed "a little odd to a republican woman to find herself in right of her country taking precedence of Marchionesses, but one soon gets used to all things"[3] — and she carefully preserved her invitations from the nobility. Bancroft showed a similar ambivalence. His diplomatic post and his reputation as a historian made him something of a social lion; without relinquishing his political distrust of the élite, Bancroft found that he enjoyed such company. He had been snubbed by the Whig aristocrats of Boston, and his wife had been forced to share his isolation; therefore, it was soothing for them both to be made much of by the more distinguished Whigs of London. His student days in Europe had given him a certain cosmopolitan polish to go with his patriotic nationalism, but he returned from this stay in Europe a confident and mature man of the world.

While in Paris, he wrote that Robespierre had possessed "a nature as incapable of respecting abilities superior to his own as George Ticknor himself."[4] Boston had many men like Ticknor, and on his return Bancroft established residence in New York City, which had shown itself readier to recognize Bancroft's superior abilities. The move also forestalled any pressures to re-involve himself in party politics. Moreover, since Bancroft had acquired a wealth of materials in Europe but had been able to write little, he returned home swearing to devote himself to the *History*, and he did so. The next decade was his most productive one as a historian.

Still a Jacksonian, strong for the Union, Bancroft was not happy with a Democratic party partly controlled by men who openly spoke of secession if the institution of slavery were threatened. Hawthorne wrote a campaign biography for Franklin Pierce, an old college classmate; but Bancroft had no very high opinion of Pierce. Over the Kansas question, "The President has been so busy reading people out of the Democratic Party, that he has at last wandered himself so far astray as to be entirely beyond hailing distance. . . . Of course he has got round him so many whigs, that democrats are crowded out of an organization pretending to the democratic name."[5] He was pleased with the 1856 nomination of James Buchanan, but he remained doubtful about the party's direction.[6] Not yet an abolitionist, Bancroft still hated slavery even more than he loved the Democratic party. When his old friend Buchanan compromised with the Southerners who had elected him, Bancroft's sympathies were therefore transferred to Stephen Douglas, the Illinois Senator who combined respect for states' rights, love of the Union, and distaste for slavery. In 1860, Bancroft happily voted for Douglas, but Douglas's large popular vote earned him only twelve electoral votes. The Southern Democrats ran a separate candidate, John Breckinridge, who carried the South; some border states went to John Bell and the Constitutional Union party. The North—and, with it, the election—went to Lincoln and the Republicans; and the South prepared to secede.

The Civil War brought out Bancroft's intense patriotism and returned him to active politics. The future eulogist of Lincoln was not at first much impressed with the new administration: "We have a president without brains; and a cabinet whose personal views outweigh patriotism."[7] A year of speaking in public on behalf of the Union and the war to preserve it did not alter his private views: Lincoln "is ignorant, self-willed, & is surrounded by men some of whom are almost as ignorant as himself. . . . How hard in order to sustain the country to sustain a man who is incompetent."[8] Such views were common at the time and did not harm Bancroft's reputation as a judge of character. Indeed, one observer wrote in 1863 that "George Bancroft has the insight of a genuine historian. Few men, if any, can be compared to him for the clearness, breadth, and justness with which in this war Bancroft comprehends and embraces events and men. Bancroft's judgment is almost faultless, and it is to be regretted that Bancroft, so to speak, is outside of the circle instead of being inside, and in some way among the pilots."[9]

Bancroft himself quite probably thought that he could have managed affairs better than Lincoln; Washington was full of men who thought themselves better than their chief, as did some cabinet members. But, however Bancroft felt, he remained on the outside. He was able to supply Lincoln with historical precedents for the suspension of *habeas corpus*, an act of which Bancroft disapproved; he also secured from Lincoln and helped publish what is now the standard text of Lincoln's Gettysburg Address. But Bancroft's chief service was as a prominent Democrat who gave the war wholehearted public support. Although he would not run for office himself, he campaigned for the Lincoln ticket in 1864.

Bancroft was one of those urging the abolition of slavery on Lincoln, and he was disappointed by the limited scope of the Emancipation Proclamation of 1863, which affected only the states in rebellion. His views on this question brought him close to the Radical Republicans in Congress and he maintained his personal friendship with one of their leaders, Charles Sumner of Massachusetts, an old acquaintance. But Bancroft felt even closer to Andrew Johnson, the Union Democrat from Tennessee who became President after the assassination of Lincoln. Johnson was a Tennessee man who, like

Bancroft, cherished the memory of Jackson. Bancroft's efforts to reconcile Sumner and Johnson were unsuccessful, and he would not choose between them. He wrote Johnson's first annual message to Congress for him in December, 1865, but this service was kept secret until revealed by a scholar some forty years later. Perhaps this aid to Johnson led to his being chosen, Edwin Stanton having refused, to deliver the official eulogy of Lincoln before a joint session of Congress in 1866. The speech cited opinions of Lincoln which were favored by both Johnson and the Radicals and which received separate bursts of applause from adherents of the differing views. In 1867, the President rewarded Bancroft by making him Minister to Prussia, an appointment which met with no opposition from the Radicals in Congress.

The appointment once again removed Bancroft from active participation in American politics, which in any case held no real place for him; he would not become a Republican, but he was no longer a partisan Democrat. Ulysses S. Grant had expressed personal approval of Bancroft's appointment, and Bancroft favored Grant for President in 1868: "Set it down as certain that my mission to Berlin is my farewell to public life. Set it down also that were the party of Seymour and Pendleton to succeed, I should at once retire."[10] In 1872, Bancroft again supported Grant: "I look upon the re-election of Grant to be certain; all just and sensible democrats will vote for him."[11] As a Johnson appointee, his main concern was to keep his post after Grant's election.

On receiving the appointment, Bancroft admitted no more to his wife than that he was "reconciled to the new position"; but he actually valued it a great deal.[12] He had studied in Germany, and his admiration for the German nation had already found expression in the *History*. He identified Otto von Bismarck's pursuit of a unified Germany with the unification of the American colonies. In the growing tension between France and Prussia, Bancroft, who had never thought much of Napoleon III, wholeheartedly supported Prussia; but his willingness to express these views in private was scarcely in keeping with the discretion to be expected of a diplomat. In late 1868, one such occasion led to an acrimonious dispute with General Dix, the American representative in Paris.

The affair not only consumed Cabinet time but also threatened Bancroft's reappointment. Never at his best in public controversy, Bancroft in his letters was "long, in bad temper, and acrimonious, and not justified even if it be admitted that Dix was wrong."[13] Another observer thought the Dix-Bancroft letters showed "The weakness of a driveler and the impertinence of a pedagogue."[14] Bancroft's pro-German prejudice was widely shared in Washington, and this factor may have saved him. When the Franco-Prussian War began, Bancroft regarded it as "one of the greatest and most momentous in the history of man. Germany represents the cause of civil and religious liberty, and her success is as devoutly to be prayed for, as ours in our war of independence, or that of Holland in its war against Phillip the Second."[15] Such strong opinions, reinforced by a personal friendship with Bismarck, made Bancroft's tenure in Berlin of more use to his hosts than to his government.

The Berlin climate was hard on Bancroft's wife, and he himself did not always find it healthy. In 1874, he resigned and sailed home to settle in Washington, D.C. Situated in that city, Bancroft could hardly avoid knowing the current political gossip, but he preferred to devote his remaining years to his writing. He wrote Matthew Arnold, a recent house guest, "In my old age I continue as in my youth to trust the people";[16] but the people's representatives in the Gilded Age aroused|no enthusiasm in a man busy chronicling the deeds of the Founding Fathers. His passions could still be aroused when conversation turned to the issues of the past, but those issues were long since resolved. Talk of a third term for Grant aroused his disapproval, and on the monetary issues of the day he remained a hard-money Jacksonian. In 1884, when the Supreme Court ruled that Congress had the constitutional power to issue paper money, Bancroft's position had already been made clear in his *Constitution* volumes; but he restated it in a pamphlet, *A Plea for the Constitution of the United States, Wounded in the House of its Guardians* (1886). This publication had no noticeable effect on public opinion, although Henry Adams expressed his gratitude for Bancroft's "saying, with dignity and weight such as no one else can command, what history requires should be said."[17] In 1879, the Senate had voted Bancroft full privileges of its floor, but it was not because he was still a political power. A man who had outlived his time, he had become a much revered but little-heeded elder statesman.

II *The Later Career of a Historian*

Bancroft's diplomatic duties slowed the writing of the *History* but gave him access to European materials untouched by previous investigators. Even the rich social life of London could be turned to his advantage in this respect. "His heart is full of manuscripts," wrote his wife to their sons—"It is the first thought I believe whoever he sees, what papers are in their family. He makes great interest with even the ladies for this purpose."[18] His visits to Paris may have produced valuable reports for his government, but Bancroft's purpose in making these trips lay elsewhere. He wrote his wife that "The Archives are so opened to me, (but this you will not speak of to anyone,) that I should commit a sin against my life, if I did not finish at least one branch of the investigation before I go home. So you must take care of the mission."[19] His standing with the liberal intellectuals of France ensured that the Revolution of 1848 did not end his access to the documents he prized. In the midst of the turmoils of a new republic, he could write that "What interests me is to see the clouds rising from over the dark passages of our history."[20]

At the end of Bancroft's service in England, he returned to America determined to make good use of these materials; and he completed in the next ten years five volumes of the *History*. He returned to find himself challenged in his own field. Richard Hildreth's three-volume *History of the United States* (1849) covered American history up to the Constitution. In many ways, Hildreth was the first important American "revisionist" historian, and his efforts to demythologize figures that Bancroft had made heroes have won him some favor from later historians. The reading public, however, continued to find Bancroft's democratic predispositions more congenial than Hildreth's more conservative biases. The difference is not simply ideological; Bancroft's sense of purpose in history gives his volumes a narrative unity lacking in Hildreth's work, though Hildreth's lines of action are as plausibly constructed.

As Bancroft's history moved into the Revolutionary era, Bancroft increasingly faced another problem, the angry descendants of men he had judged harshly. Even his old friend William Hickling Prescott expressed in advance some interest in Bancroft's treatment of his grandfather's role at the Battle of Bunker Hill, although he was well satisfied with Bancroft's eventual account.[21] Not everyone was equally pleased with Bancroft. Few good historians have been as fond of heroes as Bancroft; but, like many of his successors, he was unimpressed with the abilities of many American officers during the Revolution. A remark—which Bancroft himself later found to be inaccurate—suggesting that Joseph Reed had at one point been over-friendly with the enemy brought an angry pamphlet from William Reed, *President Reed of Pennsylvania: A Reply to George Bancroft and Others* (1867).

As usual, Bancroft, believing himself indifferent to praise or blame, asserted that he wrote out of a "sense of duty. I think I know more about the history of the epoch I am treating of, than any other person will be likely to take the trouble to do; and a *sense of duty* (mark the pride or if you will the arrogance of the statement) prompts and even compels me to go on."[2 2] But he regarded any attack on the accuracy of the *History* as one on his honor, and he responded to it with the same abrasive vigor he had shown in politics; indeed, the situation was similar, for he was once more pitted against representatives of the social élite. In the Reed case, he produced a pamphlet, *Joseph Reed, An Historical Essay*, which added a few new facts but several new and unflattering epithets, and which provoked yet another pamphlet in reply. Reed's reply contained some unflattering remarks about Benjamin Rush, which brought Rush's grandson to Bancroft's defense.

In the meantime, the grandson of Philip Schuyler had twice written Bancroft fairly polite requests for changes in the treatment of his grandfather, whose courage Bancroft had impugned. If Bancroft's reply followed his extant draft, it was unbending: historians "ought never to settle in advance with the representative of a family, the terms in which he may speak of any member of that family who has played a public part. . . . I sometimes think that you have never read my volume."[2 3] Schuyler's grandson now produced a pamphlet in defense of his ancestor, and the descendants of General Nathanael Greene and General John Sullivan also published defenses of the military virtues of their grandfathers.

Bancroft's appointment to Berlin provided him with a convenient escape from this increasingly acrimonious controversy. But the post brought him few new manuscript sources, and its duties slowed the writing of Volume X, which did not appear in print until shortly after his return to America in 1874. Even before he had finished Volume X, his publishers had suggested to him "an edition for the million."[2 4] The prospect pleased Bancroft, and on his return he set to work on what was to be the Centenary Edition of 1876-79. Although his revisions for this edition were somewhat less extensive than for the Author's Last Revision, his publishers soon became impatient. "You will bear in mind," he wrote them, "that my labors in this matter, which have been very arduous and continuous, and have occupied nearly a year, are purely labors of love, which you have not the slightest right to demand and which I shall not be able to continue after the end of the month of September."[2 5] They replied that they had anticipated only slight revisions when they had made the contract—"that we could reprint without even submitting the proofs to you. But your 'labors of love' satisfied us that it was your earnest desire, as it was certainly your interest to thoroughly revise the 8vo edition, and we were quite willing to leave the matter wholly in your hands."[26]

Free from political responsibilities and still driven by his "sense of duty," Bancroft was almost as productive in his last years as he had been in the 1850s. Even if we disregard pamphlets like *A Plea for the Constitution* (1886) and magazine contributions, the *Constitution* volumes, "The Author's Last Revision," and *Martin Van Buren* make an impressive shelf of volumes to be produced by a man already past his expected three-score-and-ten. Even before the publication of the Van Buren biography, he was projecting a life of Polk: "I propose to draw his character and especially the results of his administration; and a full and just statement of them is of great interest for the whole nation."[27] Bancroft's personal knowledge would have given this work special interest and value, but he was able to make no more than a beginning on the project. He visited Mrs. Polk in Nashville to copy materials in her possession, but the sustained effort required to complete his narrative was beyond him in his last few years. With that capacity seems to have gone much of his hold on life; his memory grew erratic, and a simple cold he had caught late in 1890 led to his death on January 17, 1891.

Bancroft cherished the contacts with the powerful that his diplomatic service brought him, but his personal friendship went to others and particularly to his fellow historians. As the friends of his youth passed away, he continued to take a sincere, if more distant, interest in his professional compeers. Until his death in 1859, William Prescott was especially close to Bancroft; and during Bancroft's mission to London, the two kept up an active correspondence. Their friendship was built on a professional respect which transcended political differences. In a passage which bears on Bancroft's own historical ideals, he writes Prescott that the distinguished French historian Augustin Thierry "spoke to me of you, as one great historian only can of another; going over the elements of historic merit; and praising not only style, and research, but the construction of your works, meaning the total form and arrangement of parts and distinct unity of the whole."[28] Prescott in return gave Bancroft high praise, although both in public and private he chided Bancroft for his failure to disclose his sources—"Every author has a right to do this, and every reader has a right to demand it."[29] But Prescott and Bancroft shared not only the common trials of historians—illegible handwriting, for example—but a common interest in combining careful research with literary quality.

Bancroft had cordial personal relations as well with the other prominent "literary" historians of mid-nineteenth-century America—Washington Irving, John Motley, and Francis Parkman. Motley had been a student at Bancroft's Round Hill, and his appointments to Vienna and London overlapped Bancroft's service in Berlin. Parkman was much younger than Bancroft, but the elder historian recognized Parkman's gifts and asked him for comments when Bancroft was preparing the Author's Last Revision. His praise of Parkman again shows the priority Bancroft gave to research in his own evaluation of historians: "You have just everything which goes to make a historian; persistency in collecting materials, indefatigable industry in using them, swift discernment of the truth, integrity and intrepidity in giving utterance to truth, a kindly humanity which is essential to the true historian and which gives the key to all hearts, and a clear and graceful and glowing manner of narration."[30]

In 1883, a young amateur named John Bach McMaster published the first volume of an American history written with Bancroft's own deep faith in the people, if perhaps not with Bancroft's concern for narrative unity. He sent Bancroft a copy, received a generous letter in reply, and soon after, evidently called on Bancroft. His report of their conversation includes a not entirely convincing explanation of why Bancroft had abandoned the use of footnotes. He quotes Bancroft as saying that McMaster's footnoting was "a mistake. At the cost of great labor you have unearthed certain facts and you tell your readers where they may find them. Some of them will use them and give you no credit. . . . All the trouble I have ever had with my books came from the notes. I am now revising them, and in the new edition there will be no notes."[31]

A new generation of historians was arising which had little use for either McMaster's amateurism of method or Bancroft's flourishes of rhetoric and which did not always distinguish between the two. The most distinguished of them was Henry Adams, who became a friendly acquaintance in Bancroft's Washington, but who wrote a rather cool review of Volume X and complained to a friend that he could not even read Bancroft's *Constitution* volumes, "though the Appendices are very entertaining."[32] If some of Bancroft's juniors found his work marred by his biases, he felt the same about some of their works; for he tactfully wrote to Henry Cabot Lodge: "I did not think your Life of Hamilton marked by that devotedness of attention and close comparison and reflection which so important a work demanded. This opinion I have never expressed except one day conversing with Henry Adams and once with my daughter-in-law. ... I venture in the purpose of real regard for you to press that idea upon you, the more so as you are now to publish what is so much needed, an edition of Hamilton's complete works."[33] And he complained to a former assistant, "The trouble of some of the younger American historians is their want of the application of the principles of historical skepticism. ... I could name one book after another whose characteristic is the careful preservation of old and long since refuted prejudices embellished and served up as valuable heirlooms."[34]

Some younger historians had trained under Bancroft himself. While in Germany, he had hired as assistants William M. Sloane and Austin Scott; both became distinguished scholars, and Scott served as president of Rutgers University.[35] Bancroft's assistants were required to do more than simply copy material—Bancroft had always hired copyists to work in various archives—for they were also assigned problems in matters of historical fact, much as a graduate student might be in a historical seminar. Familiar with most of the resources they were to use, Bancroft could give his assistants suggestions as to likely areas of search; and they could expect to be questioned closely about the results. Bancroft was ready in turn to answer their questions and, indeed, even those of strangers who made serious inquiries about points of history. His apprenticeship method of training young historians was already being replaced by the German seminar system, and his conclusions and methods were under fire from some of its advocates, but his service to his profession, as well as his achievements in it, had earned him his 1886 presidency of the fledgling American Historical Association.

III *The Rhetoric of History*

Bancroft's *History* bears the clear marks of his political philosophy, but its intent is to provide a true image of the past, and its audience is a general one since Bancroft wrote it not only for his contemporaries in America but for any who could read English and benefit from history. He had every reason to hope and expect that his work would be read with profit for years after his death. We accept this objective as the aim of every true historian, but it is obviously not the only one by which historical writing may be shaped. History may also be written to persuade a particular audience to take a particular action; since persuasive argument is the classical province of rhetoric, we may call this the "rhetoric" of history. Bancroft's first volume may have "voted for Jackson," but it was not written to persuade Americans to vote for his successors. To take a modern example, the account of President Kennedy by Arthur Schlesinger, Jr., is obviously informed with Schlesinger's personal feeling for Kennedy and his policies; but the work is written as an attempt at an objective history. Schlesinger's earlier *Kennedy vs. Nixon* is, however, an unabashed campaign tract aimed at liberal voters who failed to see 1960 as a year of real choice.

The campaign biography is, in fact, the most common example of the "rhetoric" of history in contemporary America. The genre has a surprisingly respectable history—Hawthorne did not scorn to write a campaign biography of Franklin Pierce—and in 1844 Bancroft set to work to produce a campaign biography of Martin Van Buren. The nomination of Polk made the work unnecessary as a campaign document, and Bancroft apparently did not think it of sufficient intrinsic interest at the time to see it through to publication. But in 1887 he wrote an editor that he had a manuscript complete through "the end of [Van Buren's] career as President which he could easily finish."[36] This first inquiry failed of its purpose; and the next spring, writing another editor, Bancroft himself remained unsure whether the book should be committed to print or to the fire. The reply was that it should be retained for its historical value, though only his name would give it salability, and that Harpers would probably insist on its being lengthened.[37] Harpers published the volume, *Martin Van Buren* (1889), but the biography does not take Van Buren past the end of his career as President, and there is little evidence of revision. A campaign biography published forty-five years too late, it was not, therefore, the most appropriate volume to end Bancroft's long career as a historian.[38]

Bancroft's Preface does not give the date of original composition but says that "The manuscript was seen by Van Buren," who had confirmed its accuracy (iii). His account of its subsequent history seems more than a little disingenuous: "At the time of its preparation the public mind was grievously agitated by party divisions on public affairs and on public men; the manuscript was, therefore, put aside for publication in times more favorable to a fairness of judgment on the character and career of Van Buren. In my recent revision of the original manuscript I have made no change that could affect Van Buren's approval of it as thoroughly correct" (iii-iv). If we choose to believe the second sentence of this statement—it is almost impossible to believe the first—it would seem that revision was minimal. The text's failure to consider Van Buren's career after his Presidency—his Free-Soil candid-acy of 1848 is not even mentioned—again suggests 1844 as the latest date at which Van Buren could have seen and approved the manuscript.

Bancroft's volume, which deals with Van Buren's life in six chapters, covers his early life (1782-1812), his years in the New York legislature (1812-20), his role in the convention which revised the New York state constitution (1821), his years in the United States Senate (1821-29), his service under President Jackson (1829-37), and his years as President (1837-41).

Bancroft seems to be working from limited materials in the first two chapters since we are told almost nothing about Van Buren's childhood and youth. Where we might expect to be told such details, Bancroft gives us historical background of a sort—"The country was ringing with the great principles of independence and freedom" (3). Since the Whigs had branded "Little Van" an Eastern dandy in the election of 1840, Bancroft stresses his humble origins: "Much of his future celebrity may be traced to the unpretending virtues which pervade the families of our agricultural class, and give their sons natural dignity and self-reliance" (4). His first half-dozen pages have scarcely more facts to offer—the date and place of birth, the piety of the mother and occupation of the father, the date Van Buren first began to read law (at home), and Van Buren's election as a youthful delegate to a Republican country convention in 1800. As Van Buren takes a more active role in politics, Bancroft's account becomes more detailed; but this fullness is obtained by lengthy quotation of Van Buren speeches and favorable estimates of his character. The implicit purpose of the first two chapters is to show that Van Buren's early public career was consistent with his later principles—and that he was always a man of the people.

The third chapter, an account of the 1821 constitutional con-vention, is as long as any other chapter, but its subject scarcely seems to merit it. A glance at its pages suggests that Bancroft was compensating for the meagerness of his documentation in the previous chapters by padding this chapter with material on the convention proceedings. The great achievement of the convention was extending the franchise to all white male residents—Bancroft defends Van Buren against the charge of inconsistency in supporting property restrictions on black suffrage by arguing that lack of such restrictions would have defeated the proposed amendments at the polls.

The chapters which recount Van Buren's service in the Senate, as Secretary of State, and eventually as Vice-President are, like the chapter on his service in the New York legislature, made up of public statements by Van Buren, public testimonials to him, and passages like this one: "Elevated to the second highest office in our land, his sympathies remained, as they had ever been, with the class from which he had sprung and by which he had been elevated—the more numerous and less wealthy" (177). Opposition to Van Buren before and during his Presidency is generally attributed to the machinations of the banking interests. Van Buren's difficulties as President were compounded by the Panic of 1837; Bancroft traces its economic causes without for a moment admitting that Jacksonian fiscal policy might have contributed to the crisis. Bancroft digresses to include the congressional debates during Van Buren's presidential years, and his subject is sometimes lost sight of as a result. The last few pages discuss Van Buren in retirement, but even some of these remarks seem to have been revised only by having their tenses changed—"Thus far in his career he pursued a system of progressive legislation, not rejecting the past, but, with moderation and avoiding glaring transitions, he sought to improve and reform the past" (237).

The biography is notable for its omissions, and the most regrettable of these is the lack of any account of Van Buren as a party manager. Van Buren's Albany Regency, a powerful political machine, might as well have never existed, for Van Buren is presented as a heroic figure rising to power by personal ability and public esteem. "Few statesmen have relied less on patronage," writes Bancroft, "and few public men were ever more free from personal intrigue" (236). Such a tribute may not be wholly undeserved, but no public man at that time could ignore the power of patronage and intrigue, as Bancroft himself knew well. Van Buren was one of the shrewdest politicians of his era, and the effect of Bancroft's biography is like that of reading an account of Franklin Delano Roosevelt, Lyndon Johnson, or Richard Nixon with most of the politics omitted. Bancroft's political expertise might have enabled him to write a permanently useful account of Van Buren as a political strategist, but he did not choose to do so. The reason seems obvious: the biography is not shaped by a desire to provide a rounded picture of Van Buren but by the objective of presenting those sides of Van Buren which might appeal to voters. Van Buren's reputation for political craftiness and worse was only too well established; what the task required was a view of him as a statesman marked by firm democratic principles but whose actions had sometimes been regretably misunderstood.

A campaign biography of this sort has something of the aspect of a eulogy for a man not yet dead. A leading orator and a leading politician, Bancroft was well equipped to eulogize political figures, living and dead. His eulogies of Andrew Jackson and Abraham Lincoln present their subjects as moral and political exemplars. The language and ideas are those of the *History*, but the occasion and intended audience are more restricted; in more aspects than one, they belong with the "rhetoric" of *History*.

The particular intent of the Jackson eulogy seems to be the obvious one: to praise the greatness of the man and thereby uplift the spirits of the mourners. Bancroft's "orphan boy" in the wilderness finds his destiny in the freedom of the frontier in passages which recall the earliest mentions of Washington in the *History*.[39] His public career is reviewed, defended, and praised; and Jackson's character is presented in terms that would seem to justify immediate canonization: "No man with truer instinct received American ideas; no man expressed them so completely, or so boldly, or so sincerely. He was as sincere a man as ever lived. . . . He united personal courage and moral courage beyond any man of whom history keeps the record" (219). Clearly this eulogy makes no attempt to present a rounded historical judgment; but the occasion called for such a presentation, as Bancroft suggests in lines which imply that he had been modeling his eulogy on *Julius Caesar*—"His faults and frailties have perished. Whatever of good he has done lives, and lives forever" (220).

Bancroft's eulogy of Lincoln also suppresses his personal reservations in favor of unqualified praise, but more clearly partisan aims also seem to be in evidence. The struggle between Congress and Lincoln's successor was already in progress, and Bancroft was on Johnson's side. Speaking to a joint session of Congress, Bancroft identified Lincoln with his own views; but the body of Bancroft's speech kept some sort of balance between the positions of the contending factions—his vigorous denunciation of slavery and slaveholders surely pleased the Radicals—but its peroration stresses Lincoln's agreement with the milder principles which Johnson wished to implement for the Reconstruction era: "It was the nature of LINCOLN to forgive. When hostilities ceased, he, who had always sent forth the flag with every one of its stars in the field, was eager to receive back his returning countrymen, and meditated 'some new announcement to the South.' . . . Three days before his death he declared his preference that 'the elective franchise were now conferred on the very intelligent of the

colored men, and on those of them who served our cause as soldiers;'
but he wished it done by the States themselves, and he never harbored
the thought of exacting it from a new government, as a condition of its
recognition."[40]

Bancroft then makes a long digression, a comparison of Lincoln with
Lord Palmerston, who had died soon after Lincoln; and this passage
shows that Bancroft's mission to London had not made him any sort of
Anglophile.[41] But his summary conclusion again touches on the great
issue of the day: "The States which would have left us are not brought
back as subjugated States, for then we should hold them only so long as
that conquest could be maintained; they come to their rightful place
under the Constitution as original, necessary, and inseparable members
of the Union" (50).

Pamphlets like *Joseph Reed* and *A Plea for the Constitution* are
works of the same sort: they use the materials gathered for the *History*
as ammunition in a current controversy. The first, a defense of the
History, is disfigured by Bancroft's ill temper; the second, an argument
against paper money, is a more respectable piece of writing, but it was
nearly as irrelevant when published as it seems today. Bancroft's minor
works also include a few minor historical notes and some literary
criticism; but they add no more than his Van Buren biography does to
his reputation, which must stand or fall on the *History*.

IV   The Poetics of History

The effectiveness of a political pamphlet can be judged on a single
criterion, whether or not it gains adherents for the views it advocates.
The criteria for evaluating a work like the *History* are far less clear.
Although historians sometimes profess to have little difficulty in
distinguishing "good" history from "bad," the standards employed are
vague at best and the results are not always consistent. The one obvious
demand that we make of a work like the *History* is that it be accurate
in detail—that its "facts" represent our best estimates of the truth of
the past. Even when it is possible to agree on what the historical facts
are, this criterion is a minimal one. We have already seen that a
historical narrative is more than an assemblage of true facts about the
past, and it is obvious that adding a few more facts does not make a
narrative that much better. Moreover, we continue to read with profit
historians like Bancroft and Parkman, Gibbon and Macaulay, knowing
that many of their statements of fact have since been questioned and
that historical research has since unearthed many new and significant
facts. What ends do such works serve?

Bancroft himself believed that he was demonstrating the workings of Providence and moral law in history. But we have already argued that Bancroft's beliefs do not play a causal role in his narrative and that we can accept his narrative without accepting his beliefs. Historians who argue for a particular thesis can be evaluated by examining the validity of their arguments, but we do not need to be a Whig to enjoy Macaulay, nor must we blame Christianity for the fall of Rome in order to regard Gibbon as a great historian. Our pleasure in Bancroft is only momentarily affected by our failure to respond affirmatively to passages like this one: "History is, of all pursuits, the most cheering; it throws a halo of delight and hope even over the sorrows of humanity, and finds promises of joy among the ruins of empires and the graves of nations; it sees the footsteps of Providential Intelligence everywhere, and hears the gentle tones of its voice in the hour of tranquility" (ALR, II, 324).

When we discussed the nature of historical explanation, we concluded that works like the *History* are explanatory only if we consider narrative itself a kind of explanation. To discuss the satisfactions offered by historical narratives, we must ask what makes a story a satisfactory answer to the question "Why?" We can then evaluate Bancroft's *History* by asking how well it provides this satisfaction.

In discussing the form of Bancroft's narrative, we said that its "object of imitation" was Bancroft's image of the American past. In Aristotle's *Poetics* (4, 1448b 4-24), delight in imitation is a simple fact of human nature because from imitation we learn. This leaves open the question of what we learn from a narrative like Bancroft's and why we might want to learn it. One answer has been that the vicarious experience provided by imitations of human actions enriches our understanding of the possibilities of human nature: living in comfortable suburbs, we may learn about the darker sides of our nature by reading of the atrocities in Nazi Germany or My Lai; more to the point, living in an age which assassinates its heroes, we may learn from and take pleasure in Bancroft's account of the heroes of the Revolution. But although narratives may, indeed, serve this function, it cannot be said to be one of the strengths of Bancroft's narrative, for he rarely gives us much insight into individual characters. Most individuals play a subordinate role in his narrative, and his lines of action are most convincing when his agents' behavior is well within our normal expectations of human beings.

In our discussion of narrative manner, we spoke of it as distinguished by the presence of a narrative voice. Although this voice cannot be considered explanatory, it is possible that it contributes to our pleasure in narrative. We read Gibbon partly for the pleasure we take in his style and in his personal judgments, even when we disagree with them—just as we may read a novel partly for the pleasure of coming in contact with the mind of a Fielding or a Henry James. Bancroft's rather stilted eloquence reveals a considerably less interesting mind, but it did impress some of his contemporaries as the appropriate way to speak of the great events of the American Revolution. Fortunately for modern readers, the bulk of Bancroft's narrative is carried forward in relatively unobtrusive, workmanlike prose. To our present tastes, Bancroft's *History* does not seem a notable achievement in style. In any case, this is not really an important criterion. We do not read Gibbon only for his style, and it is hard to imagine anyone reading the ten volumes of the *History* for style alone, no matter how good it might be.

Throughout this study, we have stressed that the unity of Bancroft's history is provided by a plot, composed of interdependent lines of action, leading from one essential incident to another. The essential incidents are not immediately recognizable as part of the same story—the planting of a colony does not lead automatically to that colony's declaration of independence. A narrative like Bancroft's may be said to explain these incidents by showing that one incident is linked to another by lines of action composed of many other incidents and making up a sequence of events in which each successive incident is seen as plausible in itself. The changing situations of history can then be comprehended as part of an intelligible whole.[42] The *History* easily meets this standard of historical explanation.

The intelligibility of the whole is not simply a product of the plausibility of the lines of action but of Bancroft's ability to arrange those lines of action into a plot which takes a coherent shape. In any literary form, we derive pleasure from an author's ability to create order out of experience. We may do so without believing that experience itself is ordered: A Robert Frost poem like "Design" suggests that the design of things is either malign or nonexistent, but the poem itself is a fine sonnet—that is, it imposes the human order of art upon its materials. Although we may believe in predestination or in economic determinism, the facts of history do not arrange themselves into any order until someone like Bancroft imposes his own arrangement upon them. Although we may dissent from the predispositions which enable him to do so, we can still respond to the vision of order Bancroft creates in the *History*, for history of this sort is part of man's search for symbolic forms to contain the chaos of his experience. In this case, the sheer mass of the *History* is relevant, for it is a measure of the comprehensiveness of the narrative synthesis Bancroft provides. Bancroft's research was extensive, but the great intellectual achievement of the *History* is to place the facts he found within a meaningful structure. Using narrative to create this order, Bancroft made the *History* an impressive literary achievement as well.

CHAPTER 7

Conclusion

F EW modern American intellectuals have been as successful in politics as George Bancroft. Not content to give advice from the sidelines, Bancroft relished power, and he was not too squeamish for the rough and sometimes dirty politics of his time. As Collector of the Port of Boston, he held one of the richest patronage posts of the era. As Secretary of the Navy, he was one of the most powerful men in President Polk's cabinet. It is hard to tell whether Bancroft might have achieved still more had he remained active in politics; in any case, he preferred a diplomatic career and held two of the most important diplomatic posts at his government's disposal. Although this public career took time away from Bancroft's scholarly pursuits, it gave him access to important documents for his *History*, and it allows us to feel confident that his account of political processes is based on personal experience of the ways of politics.

Bancroft was the brilliant son of a brilliant father, but it seemed at first that he might find no adequate outlet for his ambitions, for neither the ministry nor teaching suited his talents. Bancroft had been trained as a scholar; and, when he found his subject, his future was assured. The first volume of the *History* brought him immediate fame, and for fifty years he was the acknowledged master of his subject. Although his immediate successors, products of a later German school of history than Bancroft, felt the need to react against him, Bancroft's narrative helped establish what is still an important framework for understanding our early history.[1] The *History* remains an important work for those who specialize in American history. An author of important studies in the period, Daniel Boorstin, has written that to learn "what it all adds up to" one must still return to Bancroft and a handful of others.[2] Edmund S. Morgan, one of the most distinguished contemporary historians of early America, has said that Bancroft remains "in many ways the greatest" of the historians of the Revolutionary War, adding that Bancroft knew "the sources better than anyone has since."³ It seems clear that Bancroft will continue to occupy an important place in American historiography.

Bancroft's place in American literary history seems less clear, for it is not likely that he will ever again be much read for pleasure. The *History* is one of those long nineteenth-century works which, like some long narrative poems and some "triple-decker" novels, seem destined to be read mainly by college professors and their students. The one-volume abridgment now available, although useful for pedagogical purposes, can give no sense of Bancroft's achievement because it inevitably fails to convey the architecture of the whole. But read or unread, the *History* belongs to American literary history, and it must be placed and evaluated in that context.

Bancroft's most immediate affinities are naturally with the other great "literary" figures in nineteenth-century American historiography—John Motley, Francis Parkman, William Prescott, and possibly Washington Irving. Of these, only Prescott was Bancroft's equal as a historian. In *History as Romantic Art*, David Levin has argued that all of these men are literary romantics. Although this statement applies with less force to Bancroft than to his fellows, it does point to his closeness to the major drift of nineteenth-century American literature. Romanticism, of course, is a term applicable to writers of various persuasions; but Bancroft's optimism, faith in progress, democratic political philosophy, and reformism place him with Motley rather than Prescott, and with Whitman rather than Melville.

Although few would deny Thucydides a place in Greek literature, Bancroft and his fellow historians are not always accorded a place in American literary history. The dominant criticism of our time has favored poetry and those novels and plays whose density of symbolic detail permits us to use the same critical tools. We scarcely know how to deal with Emerson's essays, let alone a work like the *History*. Although historians continue to profit from the reading public's pleasure in their art, many historians today have taken our critics' concern with diction and symbol to mean that literature is a mere manner of style; since historians are only secondarily concerned with matters of style, they have been reluctant to see history treated as literature.

This study has assumed that literature is a matter of structure as well as of style, and we have argued that Bancroft's ability to comprehend his myriad details within a narrative synthesis is the secret of his strength as a historian. The beliefs which give shape to his narrative were a product of his early life and training and underlie his political career as well. The details which compose his narrative were the product of arduous research; although Bancroft's narrative voice often lacks the objectivity of tone we now prefer, we can put our trust in its substantial accuracy. Bancroft was a great master of narrative prose. The story he chose to tell will be important to us as long as America remains a great nation. The *History* tells that tale so fully and makes it so comprehensible that it won its author fame, riches, and a mass readership in his lifetime; it should also earn him an important place today in American literature as well as historiography.

Notes and References

Chapter One

1. Reported in *Magazine of American History*, XVI (1886), 619.

2. *Ibid.*

3. "On Self-Government," *Magazine of American History*, XVI (1886), 550. Future references in text.

4. Given to the New York Historical Society, November 20, 1854. Reprinted in *Literary and Historical Miscellanies* (New York, 1855), pp. 481-517—hereafter cited as *Miscellanies*.

5. David W. Noble, *Historians Against History* (Minneapolis, 1965), pp. 18-36, stresses this side of Bancroft's thought. For a less tendentious account of the historiographical background, consult George H. Callcott, *History in the United States, 1800-1850* (Baltimore, 1970).

6. Given at Williams College in August, 1835. Reprinted in *Miscellanies*, pp. 408-35.

7. *History of the Colonization of the United States* (Boston, 1834), p. vii. This became Volume I of the ten-volume *History* (Boston, 1834-76), and will be cited as such in the text.

8. In what follows and in other biographical sections of this study, I owe a special debt to Russel B. Nye, *George Bancroft, Brahmin Rebel* (New York, 1944), the standard critical biography; citations to Nye in text and notes are to this volume unless otherwise identified. Also useful is Mark DeWolfe Howe's two-volume *Life and Letters of George Bancroft* (New York, 1908). I have tried to check the original documents in all cases; but, where material is given in full by Howe I have cited it from his volume for the convenience of the reader. Most such materials not noted as available elsewhere can be found at the Massachusetts Historical Society.

9. Quoted in Howe, I, 5. The entire "Memoranda" may be found on the first of seven reels of Bancroft papers available (for rent or sale) from the Cornell University Library.

10. Letter to William B. Sprague, January 28, 1862, given in Howe, I, 7.

11. Sermon by Rev. Alonzo Hill, quoted in Howe, I, 9n.

12. Letter to Sprague (see n. 10 above).

13. Quoted in Howe, I, 33.

14. Letter to Edward Everett, August 1, 1819, at Massachusetts Historical Society.

15. Letter to Aaron Bancroft, June 6, 1821, at American Antiquarian Society, Worchester, Massachusetts.

16. Quoted in Nye, p. 64. On the relationship between Bancroft's religious views and his philosophy of history, see Russel B. Nye, "The Religion of George Bancroft," *Journal of Religion*, XIX (1939), 216-34.

17. Letter to Edward Everett, August 1, 1819, quoted in Howe, I, 65-66.

18. Letter to Jane Bancroft, November 5, 1823, at American Antiquarian Society. There are a number of useful accounts of Round Hill School, listed in the bibliography of Nye (1944); a more recent, but very slight, account is in John Walton, "The Educational Philosophy of George Bancroft," *School and Society*, LXXXII (1955), 163-65.

19. Letter to President Kirkland, August 6, 1827, quoted in Howe, I, 177-78.

20. Rev. George E. Ellis, quoted in Howe, I, 178, from the *Educational Review* of April, 1891.

21. Letters from Sarah Dwight, March 7, 1826 and March 24, 1826, at Cornell University.

22. Letter to Sarah Dwight, February 20, 1827, at Cornell.

23. For example, a letter to Sarah Bancroft, April 5, 1830, at Cornell: "My dearest Puss, I will not close my eyes tonight without writing to you, how incessantly I lament your absence, how earnestly I desire your return." Bancroft's letters to his second wife are also pleasant reading; some of those from the Cornell collection are exploited in Patricia Clark, " 'A Tale to Tell from Paradise Itself': George Bancroft's Letters from Florida, March 1855," *Florida Historical Quarterly*, XLVIII (1970), 264-78.

24. Andrew Schiller, "A Letter from George Bancroft," *New England Quarterly*, XXXIII (1960), 225-32, reports on a letter (in Schiller's possession) from Bancroft to an unknown party in September, 1823, making light of the soon-to-be-published *Poems* and enclosing some verse. Schiller also catches Bancroft in the *Poems*, taking two lines from Goethe's "Mignon" for his "Rome."

25. See Nye, "George Bancroft, Early Critic of German Literature," *Modern Language Notes*, LVIII (1943), 128-36, and O. W. Long, "Goethe and Bancroft," *Studies in Philology*, XXVIII (1931), 288-97.

26. Edward Everett to Jared Sparks, October 6, 1828, at Massachusetts Historical Society. On Bancroft's work for the *American Quarterly*, see Guy R. Woodall, "A Reviewer and His Editor: The Literary Relationship of George Bancroft and Robert Walsh," *Tennessee Studies in Literature*, XIV (1969), 35-50.

27. Letters from Jared Sparks, December 11, 1826, and January 2, 1827, quoted in Howe, I, 183n. See also John Spencer Bassett, "The Correspondence of George Bancroft and Jared Sparks, 1823-1832," *Smith College Studies in History*, II:2 (1917).

28. Edward Everett to Alexander Everett, August 6, 1830, at Massachusetts Historical Society.

29. Second American edition published as *Ancient Greece* (Boston, 1842), p. vi. References in text to this edition. The Harvard edition was apparently arranged by Jared Sparks—Sparks, letter to Bancroft, October 2, 1841, at Massachusetts Historical Society: "I have recommended to the Corporation your translation of Heeren's politics of Greece as a college book, and they have concluded to adopt it.

30. *History of the Political System of Europe* (Northampton, Mass., 1828), I, 8. References in text to this edition. On Heeren's influence see Fred L. Burwick, "The Göttingen Influence on George Bancroft's Idea of Humanity," *Jahrbuch für Amerikastudien*, XI (1966), 194-212, which discusses the effect of Bancroft's contact with Heeren, Johann Eichhorn, and Johann Blumenbach.

31. *History of the States of Antiquity* (Northampton, Mass., 1828), p. iv. Future references in text.

32. Letter to President Kirkland, March 5, 1828. See also letter to Kirkland, February 3, 1828, and letter from George Ticknor, March 24, 1828. All letters at Massachusetts Historical Society.

33. The relatively minor role played by abstract ideas in the *History* is noted by both John Higham, *Writing American History* (Bloomington, 1970), pp. 43-44, and Robert Allen Skotheim, *American Intellectual Histories and Historians* (Princeton, 1966), pp. 15-18.

34. W. H. Walsh, *Introduction to the Philosophy of History* (London, 1951), p. 51. Walsh regards this use of "leading ideas" as in itself at least a partial form of "explanation"—calling it "colligation"—but this further claim is not involved here.

35. The use of "narrative frame of reference" here reflects Haskell Fain, *Between Philosophy and History: The Resurrection of Speculative Philosophy of History Within the Analytic Tradition* (Princeton, 1970).

36. See Morton White, *The Foundations of Historical Knowledge* (New York, 1965), pp. 271-91, for a discussion of this point by a philosopher who does believe that historical narratives necessarily imply causal chains.

37. Even in fiction, we may argue that we gain from an explicit statement of the author's value system, a point basic to Wayne Booth's *The Rhetoric of Fiction* (Chicago, 1961). In a historical work, we may even have the right to demand it—though perhaps not at Bancroft's length.

38. For background see Leroy Moore, Jr., "Roger Williams and the Historians," *Church History*, XXXII (1963), 432-51, although Moore spends little time on Bancroft.

39. George D. Langdon, Jr., "The Franchise and Political Democracy in Plymouth Colony," *William & Mary Quarterly*, XX (1963), 513-26, concludes that Bancroft was right in seeing that colony as essentially democratic. The degree of democracy in Massachusetts as a whole is still a matter of lively interest, and Bancroft's democratic emphasis still has its defenders. One of the most aggressive is Robert E. Brown; on a later period, see his *Middle-Class Democracy and the Revolution in Massachusetts, 1691-1780* (Ithaca, 1955) and, for a specific defense of Bancroft, *Carl Becker on History and the American Revolution* (East Lansing, 1970), pp. 141-42.

Chapter Two

1. Letter from John Davis, April 2, 1835, in Howe, I, 210-11.

2. Letter from Everett, October 5, 1833, in Howe, I, 206-207.

3. Quoted in Howe, I, 186.

4. Letter to Sarah Dwight, July 1, 1826, at Cornell.

5. Letter to Edward Everett, February 7, 1835, at Massachusetts Historical Society. Since the Whig élite was prepared to receive Bancroft, it would seem unfair to interpret such remarks as evidence of political opportunism. Bancroft is charged with this and other failings in John Lukacs, "Bancroft: The Historian as Celebrity," *American Heritage*, XII:6 (October 1961), 65-68. Writing for the general reader, Lukacs offers no real evidence against Bancroft.

6. Letter from John Davis, June 27, 1830, at Cornell—mostly taken up with humorous praise of Bancroft's self-denial.

7. Letter to Sarah Bancroft, May 5, 1831, at Cornell.

8. Letter to Sarah Bancroft, May 5, 1831, at Cornell—this passage is cited in Howe, I, 189.

9. Letter from Henry Dwight, December 24, 1830, at Cornell. This letter is reprinted in Harry N. Scheiber, "Some Documents on Jackson's Bank War," *Pennsylvania History*, XXX (1963), 46-54. For further information on Bancroft's banking career, see three other articles by Scheiber: "The Commercial Bank of Lake Erie," *Business History Review*, XL (1966), 47-65, which discusses Bancroft's role in the reorganization of a Cleveland bank; "George Bancroft and the Bank of Michigan," *Michigan History*, XLIV (1960), 82-95; and "A Jacksonian

as Banker and Lobbyist: New Light on George Bancroft," *New England Quarterly*, XXXVII (1964), 363-72, an important survey of Bancroft's activities on behalf of the Dwight family's (and his own) banking interests.

10. Letter from Alexander Everett, March 26, 1831, at Massachusetts Historical Society. Compare with letter from John Davis, January 15, 1831, at Cornell.

11. Letter to Lucretia Bancroft, January 1, 1832, at American Antiquarian Society.

12. Letter to Sarah Bancroft, January 18, 1832, at Cornell, quoted in Howe, I, 201.

13. Letter to Edward Everett, October 23, 1833, at Massachusetts Historical Society.

14. See letters from Joseph Story, April 26, 1834, and May 15, 1834; from James Savage, May 25, 1834; from John C. Calhoun, June 29, 1834; and letter to Edward Everett, June 20, 1834; all letters at Massachusetts Historical Society.

15. Oration at Springfield, Mass., July 4, 1836, quoted in Howe, I, 216.

16. Amos Lawrence to Amos A. Lawrence (son), November 15, 1836, at Massachusetts Historical Society.

17. Letter to Ralph Waldo Emerson, February 29, 1836—see similar remarks in letters to Edward Everett, December 29, 1834, and February 2, 1835. All letters at Massachusetts Historical Society.

18. Letter from Orestes Brownson, November 10, 1837, at Cornell. See also C. Carroll Hollis, "Brownson on George Bancroft," *South Atlantic Quarterly*, LX (1950), 42-52.

19. Letter from Marcus Morton, December 25, 1837, at Massachusetts Historical Society.

20. Letter from William H. Prescott, January 12, 1838, at Massachusetts Historical Society; see also, letter from John Davis, February 2, 1838, at Cornell. On Bancroft's help in securing a good reception for Prescott's volume, see C. Harvey Gardiner, "Promoting a Book: Prescott to Bancroft, December 20, 1837," *Papers, Bibliographical Society of America*, LI (1957), 335-39 and Gardiner, *William Hickling Prescott* (Austin, 1969), pp. 137, 148.

21. Note in Bancroft's hand on letter from Prescott, January 12, 1838, at Massachusetts Historical Society.

22. The problems of the Bank of Michigan are the subject of a lengthy correspondence, to be found at Cornell, between Bancroft, Henry Dwight, William Dwight, and various government officials. Nye, p. 113, is too strong in saying that Sarah's death "severed his last connection with the Dwights and business," although Bancroft ceased then to gain much from the Dwight association. Besides the Scheiber

articles (n. 9 above) we might note a long correspondence, in the
Cornell collection, between Bancroft and William and Edmund Dwight,
trustees administering Sarah's father's estate. Bancroft felt that the will
indicated regular payments for support and education of his children by
Sarah; the Dwights, who felt that the money was not required by
Bancroft, preferred to apply it to the principal awaiting the children's
coming of age. Neither side appears to great advantage in this dispute.
Bancroft later tried and failed to get additional sums from the Dwights
for his services as agent for the Bank of Michigan. For another use of
Bancroft's political influence, see Ralph M. Aderman, "The Case of
James Cook: A Study of Political Influence in 1840," *Essex Institute
Historical Collections*, XCII (1956), 59-67. In 1837, a French-Canadian
rebel even wrote Bancroft in an effort to secure United States support.
This letter, to which Bancroft sent a politely negative reply has
spawned *two* articles: Ronald F. Howell, "The Political Testament of
Papineau in Exile, 1837," *Canadian Historical Review*, XXXVIII
(1957), 295-300, and Lillian F. Gates, "A Canadian Rebel's Appeal to
George Bancroft," *New England Quarterly*, XLI (1968), 96-104.

23. Copy of letter, Elizabeth Bliss to Mrs. Rebecca Parker, undated
(probably early summer, 1838) at Library of Congress.

24. Letter from Elizabeth Bancroft, December 20, 1838, at Cornell.

25. Letter to Charles Edward Lester, April 1, 1844, at Huntington
Library.

26. Draft of letter to J. T. Buckingham, December 4, 1844, at
Massachusetts Historical Society.

27. Letter from Little and Brown, April 15, 1844, at Cornell.

28. Letter to Elizabeth Bancroft, May 20, 1844, at Library of
Congress, refers to reading over "the six books of my epic poem"; this
is probably the undated, unsigned poem in the Library of Congress
Bancroft papers entitled "The Excursiad: an Epic Poem in six cantos,"
an iambic pentameter account of two children caught in a rainstorm.

29. Letter to Elizabeth Bancroft, September 30, 1844, in response
to a letter from Elizabeth Bancroft, September 18, 1844, both at
Cornell. See two earlier letters to her, May 25 and August 13, 1844,
both at Library of Congress, in which Bancroft complains that she
writes him of politics when he wants words of affection and advises her
not to worry about elections and politicians.

30. Letter to Elizabeth Bancroft, March 15, 1845, at Cornell—copy
at Massachusetts Historical Society.

31. Letter to S. A. Allibone, October 11, 1856, at Huntington
Library.

32. Of interest here is an unpublished dissertation (Utah, 1968) by
Merrill E. Lewis, "American Frontier History as Literature: Studies in
the Historiography of George Bancroft, Frederick Jackson Turner, and

Theodore Roosevelt," the source of the Lewis article cited in the bibliography below.

Chapter Three

1. Carl Becker, *Detachment and the Writing of History*, ed. Phil L. Snyder (Ithaca, 1958), p. 48. The essay quoted ("What Are Historical Facts?") has been widely reprinted. It should be noted that one can acknowledge the mental status of historical facts without necessarily committing oneself to a form of historical relativism.

2. The term "synthetic unity" is taken from W. H. Dray, "On the Nature and Role of Narrative in Historiography," *History and Theory*, X (1971), 153-71, an article which offers a convenient discussion of "narrativist" approaches to the critical philosophy of history.

3. For a more extended discussion of the "literary" dimensions of accuracy and structure in historical narratives, see David Levin, "The Literary Criticism of History," *In Defense of Historical Literature* (New York, 1967), pp. 1-33.

4. On the use of the story-plot distinction in historiography, see Hayden White, "The Structure of Historical Narrative," *CLIO*, I:3 (June, 1972), 5-20. We need not agree with Robert Scholes and Robert Kellogg that the historian who adopts the plot form must "sacrifice science to art"—see their *The Nature of Narrative* (New York, 1966), p. 217, and our discussion of historical explanation in Chapter Five below. The term "scene" in this section comes from Kenneth Burke; this chapter also owes much to the criticism of Elder Olson, especially *Tragedy and the Theory of Drama* (Detroit, 1961).

5. See J. H. Hexter, *The History Primer* (New York, 1971), p. 207.

6. Kenneth Burke, *A Grammar of Motives* (Cleveland, 1962 [1945]), p. 59.

7. *Anatomy of Criticism* (Princeton, 1957), pp. 187, 181.

8. See Morton White, *Foundations*, pp. 229-70. My "essential incidents" are much like White's "basic statements."

9. The British diplomats in Europe were closer to home and thus more subject to close supervision by their government; unlike the American diplomats, they are rarely treated in the *History* as a separate line of action.

10. Of special interest is David Levin's chapter on "Representative Men" in *History as Romantic Art* (Stanford, 1959).

Chapter Four

1. Russel B. Nye has done a very useful abridgment of Bancroft's *History* (1 vol.; Chicago, 1966) for the University of Chicago "Classic American Historians" series. Except for one chapter from the *Constitution* volumes, the selections are taken from the six-volume

1876 revision, the Centenary Edition. Included are the chapters on
Lexington and Concord dealt with in this chapter—they also appear as
appendices to Nye's 1944 biography of Bancroft.

2. "Diary of Sidney George Fisher, 1860," *Pennsylvania Magazine
of History and Biography*, LXXXVII (1963), 332, entry for March 23,
1860. Fisher was an intellectual Philadelphia aristocrat. His diaries are
available in book form as *A Philadelphia Perspective*, ed. Nicholas B.
Wainwright (Philadelphia, 1967).

3. Bancroft, *History of the Formation of the Constitution of the
United States of America* (2 vols.; New York, 1882)—cited in the text
as *Constitution* where necessary for clarity.

4. The rough drafts referred to in this section are in the Bancroft
papers at the New York Public Library. Anyone interested in Bancroft's
handling of his sources will want to consult Richard C. Vitzthum's fine
article, "Theme and Method in Bancroft's *History of the United
States*," *New England Quarterly*, XLI (1968), 362-80. Also useful is
Ronald Joseph Oard, "Bancroft and Hildreth: A Critical Evaluation,"
an unpublished Ph.D. dissertation, St. Louis University, 1961.

5. The degree to which economic and other considerations are
important has remained a matter of debate, and the economic
determinism associated with Charles Beard is by no means generally
accepted today—cf. Robert E. Brown, *Charles Beard and the
Constitution* (New York, 1965) and Jackson T. Main, *The
Antifederalists* (New York, 1961). But Bancroft's view of the
Antifederalists is clearly distorted.

6. Devotees of mythic criticism may note that Washington becomes
a fertility god of sorts: in 1779, "He has no consolation but in the hope
of a good federal government. His growing desire has the character of a
force of nature, which from the opening year increases in power till the
earth is renewed" (I, 19).

7. Dealing with the events of 1785, Bancroft gives a more favorable
account of Lee and his objections to the regulation of commerce—lists
his objections, cites his "courteous manner," and says he was
"consistent" in his views and argued with "earnest frankness" (I, 196).

Chapter Five

1. Bancroft, *History of the United States of America, from the
Discovery of the Continent* ("The Author's Last Revision," 6 vols.;
New York, 1883-85).

2. This change, like some others dealt with in this section, had been
made in previous editions of Volume VII, the pages on Vermont and
Delaware, for example, being bound in as 271a, etc. "The Author's Last
Revision" is dealt with here as the final embodiment of all Bancroft's
revisions.

3. "But duty is bolder than theory, more confident than the understanding, older and more imperative than speculative science; existing from eternity, and recognized in its binding force from the first morning of creation" (VII, 301; cf. ALR, IV, 160) and "The American revolution did not proceed from precarious intentions" (*ibid.*). A good deal of rhetoric remains uncut in this section.

4. The most practical issue involved in this debate is whether historians should be administratively grouped with the Humanities or the Social Sciences, and a good many practicing historians show little interest in such questions. Perhaps because there is little in the way of a developed philosophy of social science, the art versus social science debate has not displayed much philosophic sophistication, with the result that the antagonists have rarely come to grips with the underlying assumptions of either side.

5. So common are historical narratives unified by plot that both historians and philosophers are apt to identify narrative with plot, a practice quite rightly objected to by Hayden White in the essay cited earlier. In this study, the assumption has been that narrative is a manner of presentation distinguished by the narrative voice openly addressing the reader, a manner which contrasts with the dramatic or lyric manners. The "chronicle" versus "narrative" distinction made in Chapter 3 above is sometimes, following Croce, stated as a difference between "chronicle" and "history proper," a treatment which obscures the difference between methods of inquiry and of presentation, and is needlessly pejorative to boot. The argument that historical explanations necessarily follow models in the natural sciences is associated with the name of Carl Hempel. Hempel's 1942 article on "The Function of General Laws in History" is conveniently reprinted in Patrick Gardiner, ed. *Theories of History* (New York, 1959), pp. 345-56, and in Ronald H. Nash, ed., *Ideas of History* (New York, 1969), II, 79-106 (a revised version). See also his 1962 essay on "Explanation in Science and in History" in William H. Dray, ed., *Philosophical Analysis and History* (New York, 1966), pp. 95-126. Readers interested in following the progress of this debate can consult the general collections just cited, as well as other works cited in these notes.

6. The phrase "causal chain" comes from Morton White, *Foundations*. For a distinguished historian's rather negative reaction to White's book (and similar arguments), see J. H. Hexter, pp. 148-74.

7. It would not be fair to object that these generalizations represent mere statistical probabilities, for the same is true of many acknowledged scientific laws.

8. The reference to "re-thinking" refers to R. G. Collingwood's famous *The Idea of History* (London, 1946). The argument for explanation by motivating reasons is well presented by William H. Dray,

Laws and Explanation in History (Oxford, 1957). For arguments that reasons and causes are not fundamentally distinct, see Morton White, *Foundations*, pp. 182-218, and the 1962 article of Carl Hempel cited in note 5 above. In *The Nature of Historical Thinking* (Chapel Hill, 1967), Robert Stover argues persuasively that deterministic natural order thinking and rational agency "living-in-the-world" thinking are distinct but compatible forms of historical thought, both of which may exist within a given narrative. Stover's willingness to distinguish between "historical thinking" and its narrative presentation avoids a number of problems in other treatments of this question.

9. Arthur C. Danto, *Analytical Philosophy of History* (Cambridge, 1965), considers the possibility that particular events may prove to be instances of more than one general description (pp. 228-29) but simply assumes that such instances will be examples of overdetermination or will disappear when we find the "correct explanatum." This ignores the ambiguity of narratives. An admirer of Danto's, L. B. Cebik, discusses the complex relationship between "Narratives and Arguments," in *CLIO*, I:1 (October 1971), 7-25, concluding as we have here that a given narrative may imply several, potentially inconsistent arguments. Readers familiar with the work in semantics of generative linguists will have noted that, as linguists attempt to state the deep structure of sentences in terms approximating those of symbolic logic, multiple ambiguity begins to seem characteristic of almost every sentence.

10. W. B. Gallie, *Philosophy and the Historical Understanding* (2nd ed.; New York, 1968), avoids the term "explanation" but deals well with story as the essential element in historical narrative. Bancroft's own formulation resembles what Dray, *Laws and Explanations*, p. 66, calls the "continuous series" model, in which an event is explained by being broken down into a series of smaller events until it is somehow seen as immediately intelligible. I believe, however, that at least a loose notion of plausibility is useful in discussing both literary and historical narratives.

Chapter Six

1. J. G. Harris to Bancroft, April 10, 1887, at New York Public Library; Bancroft, Letter to William L. Stone, August 21, 1887, at Massachusetts Historical Society.

2. Letter to Elizabeth Bancroft, April 21, 1848, at Library of Congress.

3. Copy of letter, Elizabeth Bancroft to uncle, November 17, 1846, at Library of Congress. Selections from her 1846-49 letters home were published as *Letters from England* (New York, 1904).

4. Letter to Elizabeth Bancroft, April 11, 1847, at Cornell—copy at Massachusetts Historical Society.

5. Letter to W. L. Marcy (Secretary of State), September 24, 1856, in Howe, II, 123.

6. Stepson William D. Bliss, letter to Bancroft, November 16, 1865, at Library of Congress , says he is "gratified at learning that your and my political views and opinions were not far asunder; though your personal friendship for Mr. Buchanan and long and intimate knowledge of his views and abilities, might prompt you to vote in a different way from myself."

7. Letter to Elizabeth Bancroft, September 14, 1861, at Cornell.

8. Letter to Francis Lieber, October 29, 1862, at Huntington Library.

9. Count Adam Gurowski, *Diary*, II (New York, 1964), 190, entry for April 6, 1863.

10. Letter to Alexander Bliss, June 24, 1868, at Library of Congress. Horatio Seymour was the Democratic presidential candidate. Congressman Pendleton was the advocate of the "Ohio Idea," backed in the party platform, of paying off the national debt in greenbacks—and Bancroft hated the idea of paper money.

11. Letter to Elizabeth Bancroft, August 29, 1872, at Cornell.

12. Letter to Elizabeth Bancroft, August 16, 1866, at Library of Congress.

13. *Diary of Orville Hickman Browning*, II (*Collections of the Illinois State Historical Society*, XXII; Lincoln Series, III), 235, entry for January 19, 1869, on Cabinet discussion of the correspondence.

14. Howard K. Beale, ed., *Diary of Gideon Welles*, III (New York, 1960), 521, entry for February 5, 1869.

15. Letter to Elizabeth Bancroft [1870?], at Library of Congress. Arnold Blumberg, "George Bancroft, France, and the Vatican: Some Aspects of American, French, and Vatican Diplomacy," *Catholic Historical Review*, L (1965), 475-93, covers reactions to Bancroft's open Germanophilism. Henry Blumenthal dismisses its influence on Grant administration policies in his "George Bancroft in Berlin: 1867-1874," *New England Quarterly*, XXXVII (1964), 224-41. Discussing Bancroft's principal achievement while in Berlin, Lucinda Meyer, "German-American Migration and the Bancroft Naturalization Treaties, 1868-70," an unpublished Ph.D. dissertation, City University of New York, 1970, sees the treaties as badly drawn, not much used, and partly responsible for the second-class legal status assigned naturalized citizens. Mary Phillip Trauch, "The Bancroft Dispatches on the Vatican Council and the *Kulturkampf*," *Catholic History Review*, XL (1954), 178-90, stresses Bancroft's anti-Catholic bias.

16. Letter to Matthew Arnold, December 26, 1883, at Massachusetts Historical Society.

17. Henry Adams, letter to Bancroft, February 11, 1886, in *Letters of Henry Adams*, I (New York, 1930), 364.

18. Elizabeth Bancroft, letter of January 1, 1847, copy at Library of Congress.

19. Letter to Elizabeth Bancroft, April 4, 1847, at Massachusetts Historical Society.

20. Letter to Elizabeth Bancroft, February 10, 1849, at Library of Congress.

21. William Prescott, letter to Bancroft, February 19, 1852, solicits Bancroft's views on the battle in reference to a local dispute about a proposed monument. Unwilling to prejudge the matter, even for a friend, Bancroft noted at the bottom of Prescott's letter, "In answer to this I wrote that I thought I had better reserve the expression of an opinion, till I should do it in the history." When he had written his account, he sent it to Prescott, who replied, April 3, 1858, expressing his gratification with it. Both letters are at the Massachusetts Historical Society.

22. Letter to William Prescott, November 24, 1854, copy at Massachusetts Historical Society.

23. Letter to George L. Schuyler, February 5, 1867—draft at Massachusetts Historical Society—in reply to letters from Schuyler dated January 16, 1867, and February 4, 1867, both at Massachusetts Historical Society.

24. Letter to Little, Brown & Co., July 7, 1869, at Massachusetts Historical Society—Bancroft's reply to a proposal for a six-volume edition.

25. Letter to Little, Brown & Co., August 20, 1875, at Massachusetts Historical Society. At the end of September, Bancroft would be leaving his summer home in Newport, which was near the Stereotype.

26. Little, Brown & Co. to Bancroft, c. September 1, 1875, at Massachusetts Historical Society.

27. Letter to J. G. Harris, April 8, 1887, at New York Public Library.

28. Letter to William Prescott, May 18, 1847, copy at Massachusetts Historical Society.

29. William Prescott to Bancroft, March 5, 1852, at Massachusetts Historical Society. Prescott's complaint has been echoed by many later Bancroft critics. In a later letter—May 1, 1858, at Massachusetts Historical Society—he relents enough to tell Bancroft that the lack of notes may actually give the work a brisker movement, adding, "You have so long been the high priest of American history, that you can afford to become your own authority. . . . I think it would be well for you to give the public some day an account of the authorities which you use, as you propose to do in the preface."

30. Letter to Francis Parkman, November 28, 1884. For Bancroft seeking help on his revisions, see letters to Parkman, June 1, 1882, and July 27, 1882. All three letters at Massachusetts Historical Society.

31. Quoted in Eric F. Goldman, *John Bach McMaster* (Philadelphia, 1943), pp. 117-18. Bancroft's letter to McMaster is dated April 11, 1883, at Massachusetts Historical Society.

32. Henry Adams to Henry Cabot Lodge, October 31, 1882, in *Letters of Henry Adams*, I, 342. The context of this remark is important: Adams also speaks of the disgust he feels for his own work; and he is busy apologizing for his inability to read Lodge's book on Hamilton.

33. Letter to Henry Cabot Lodge, December 26, 1884, at Massachusetts Historical Society.

34. Letter to Austin Scott, February 18, 1885, at Massachusetts Historical Society.

35. Of particular interest is a detailed draft of "Instructions for Austin Scott," dated September 12, 1878, at Massachusetts Historical Society.

36. Letter to John J. Morse, Jr., August 15, 1887, at Massachusetts Historical Society.

37. William Allen Butler to Bancroft, May 11, 1888, Bancroft had sent the manuscript to Butler the previous fall—letter to Butler, October 17, 1887—and later asked Butler whether it should be printed or burned—letter to Butler, May 10, 1888. All three letters at Massachusetts Historical Society.

38. This material on how the manuscript came to print is included as evidence of its rhetorical intent. Nye, p. 300, gives a somewhat different account, indicating that Bancroft had only a "half-completed manuscript," which he added to, "working from notes more than forty years old," but agrees that the result is "an outdated campaign biography."

39. Bancroft's eulogy is prominently included in John S. Jenkins, ed., *Life and Public Services of Gen. Andrew Jackson* (New York, 1860), pp. 196-220. The "orphan boy" reference is on p. 197. The resemblance to Bancroft's remarks on Washington is noted (and objected to) by the anonymous Whig author of a pamphlet, *To George Bancroft, Secretary of the Navy, the Traducer and Eulogist of General Andrew Jackson* (Washington, 1846), pp. 13-15.

40. *Memorial Address on the Life and Character of Abraham Lincoln* (Washington, 1866), pp. 46-47.

41. See Arnold Blumberg, "Bancroft's Eulogy of Lincoln and British Reaction," *Lincoln Herald*, LXVII (1965), 151-57. For Continental reaction see the Blumberg article cited above (n. 15).

42. See Louis Mink, "History and Fiction as Modes of Comprehension," *New Literary History*, I (1970), 541-58, and the

works cited earlier of Dray, Gallie, and Hayden White. On history as man's attempt to "transcend transcience," see David F. Trask, "A Note on Relevance and History," CLIO, I:3 (June 1972), 34-39.

Chapter Seven

1. That Bancroft helped define the issues for future historians is suggested by the very title of Bert James Loewenberg's chapter, "George Bancroft: The Making of a Tradition," *American History in American Thought* (New York, 1972), pp. 239-57. This admirable survey of American historiography was published too recently for full use in this study.

2. Daniel Boorstin, *The Americans: The Colonial Experience* (New York, 1958), p. 375.

3. Edmund S. Morgan, *The Birth of the Republic, 1763-1789* (Chicago, 1956), p. 158. More negative views of Bancroft's achievements are sometimes expressed by modern historiographers. Some of these have been cited elsewhere in these notes; we may also note J. R. Pole, "The American Past: Is It Still Usable?" *Journal of American Studies*, I (1967), 63-78, and Page Smith, "David Ramsay and the Causes of the American Revolution," *William & Mary Quarterly*, XVII (1960), 51-77, an essay later incorporated in Smith's *The Historian and History* (New York, 1964), pp. 165-99. The negative stereotypes seem based more on Bancroft's philosophic pronouncements than on his actual narrative.

Selected Bibliography

PRIMARY SOURCES

1. *Separate Publications* (listed chronologically)

Poems. Cambridge, Mass.: Hilliard and Metcalf, 1823.

(With Joseph Cogswell) *Prospectus of a School to be Established at Round Hill, Northampton, Massachusetts*. Cambridge, Mass.: Hilliard and Metcalf, 1823.

(Buttmann) *A Greek Grammar*. Boston: Cummings, Hilliard, and Co., 1824.

(Heeren) *Reflections on the Politics of Ancient Greece*. Boston: Little, Brown, and Co., 1824.

(Jacobs) *The Latin Reader*. Northampton, Mass.: Shepard and Co., 1825.

(With Joseph Cogswell) *Some Account of the School for the Liberal Education of Boys*. Northampton, Mass.: Shepard and Co., 1826.

An Oration Delivered on the Fourth of July. Northampton, Mass.: Shepard and Co., 1826.

(Bremi) *Cornelius Nepos, "De Vita Excellentum Imperatorum."* Boston: Cummings, Hilliard, and Co., 1826.

(Heeren) *History of the States of Antiquity*. Northampton, Mass.: Shepard and Co., 1828.

(Heeren) *A History of the Political Systems of Europe*. New York: Butler and Carvill, 1828.

(Zumpt) *A Latin Grammar*. New York: Carvill, 1829.

The History of the United States from the Discovery of the Continent. Ten volumes; Boston: Little, Brown, and Co., 1834-1875.

An Oration Delivered Before the Democracy of Springfield, Mass., and Neighboring Towns. Boston: Merriam, 1836.

Address at Hartford, Conn., Before the Delegates to the Democratic Convention of the Young Men of Connecticut. Boston: n.p., 1840.

An Oration Delivered at the Commemoration in Washington of the Death of Andrew Jackson. Washington, D.C.: Government Printing Office, 1845.

Literary and Historical Miscellanies. New York: Harper, 1855.
On the Exchange of Prisoners during the American War of Independence. New York: New-York Historical Society, 1862.
Oration of the 22nd of February, 1862. New York: Barker, 1862.
Memorial Address on the Life and Character of Abraham Lincoln. Washington, D.C.: Government Printing Office, 1866.
Joseph Reed, An Historical Essay. New York: Middleton, 1867.
Nathanael Greene. Boston: Ticknor and Field, 1867.
Memorial on Canal de Haro as the Boundary Line of the United States of America. Berlin: Decker, 1872.
The History of the United States of America, A Centenary Edition (revised). Six volumes; Boston: Little, Brown, and Co., 1876-1879.
History of the Formation of the Constitution of the United States of America. Two volumes; New York: Appleton, 1882.
The History of the United States of America, The Author's Last Revision. Six volumes; New York: Appleton, 1883-1885.
A Plea for the Constitution of the United States, Wounded in the House of its Guardians. New York: Harper, 1886.
Martin Van Buren to the End of His Public Career. New York: Harper, 1889.
The History of the Battle of Lake Erie and Miscellaneous Papers. Edited by Oliver Dyer. New York: Robert Bonner's Sons, 1891.
The History of the United States of America. Edited and abridged in one volume from the Centenary Edition by Russel B. Nye. Chicago: U. of Chicago, 1966.

2. *Other Bancroft Publications*

This selective listing includes only items of substantial literary or historical interest. Readers requiring a more complete bibliography should begin by consulting Russel Nye, *George Bancroft* (New York, 1944) pp. 327-30.

"Schiller's Minor Poems." *North American Review*, XVI (1823), 268-80.
"Buttmann's *Greek Grammar*." *North American Review*, XVIII (1824), 99-105.
"Jacob's *Greek Reader*." *North American Review*, XVIII (1824), 280-84.
"The Value of Classical Learning." *North American Review*, XIX (1824), 125-37.
"Goethe's *Werke*." *North American Review*, XIX (1824), 303-25.
"Herder's Writings." *North American Review*, XX (1825), 138-47.
"German Literature." *American Quarterly Review*, II (1827), 171-86.

"German Literature." *American Quarterly Review*, III (1828), 150-73.
"German Literature." *American Quarterly Review*, IV (1828), 157-90.
"Taylor's *German Poetry*." *American Quarterly Review*, VII (1830), 436-49.
"The Bank of the United States." *North American Review*, XXXII (1831), 21-64.
"Boeckh's *Economy of Athens*." *North American Review*, XXXII (1831), 344-67.
"German Poetry." *American Quarterly Review*, X (1831), 194-210.
"Slavery in Rome." *North American Review*, XXXIX (1834), 413-37.
"Clark & Force, *A Documentary History of the Revolution*." *North American Review*, XLVI (1838), 475-87.
"On the Progress of Civilization." *Boston Quarterly Review*, I (1838), 389-407.
"A Memoir of Washington." *Eclectic Review*, IV (1838), 489-518.
"William Ellery Channing." *Democratic Review*, XII (1843), 524-26.
"A Tribute to Humboldt." *Pulpit and Rostrum*, VI (1859), 63-65.
"Washington Irving." *Living Age*, LXV (1860), 620-21.
"The Place of Abraham Lincoln in History." *Atlantic Magazine*, XV (1865), 757-70.
"Letter to the Editors, in Reply to a Pamphlet Concerning General Greene." *North American Review*, CIV (1867), 662-74.
"A Tribute to Whittier." *Literary World*, VIII (1877), 122.
"Holmes' *Life of Emerson*." *North American Review*, CXXXX (1885), 129-43.
"A Few Words about Henry Clay." *Century Magazine*, XXX o.s. (1885), 479-81.
"Lowell, Our Ablest Critic." *Literary World*, XVI (1885), 217-18.
"The Seventh Petition." *New Princeton Review*, I (1886), 342-45.
"On Self-Government." *Magazine of American History*, XVI (1886), 550-54.
"An Incident in the Life of John Adams." *Century Magazine*, XXXIV (1887), 434-40.

SECONDARY SOURCES

Only the most significant discussions of Bancroft's work as a historian are included here. Many additional items of secondary or strictly biographical interest are listed in the Notes and References.

DANZER, GERALD A. "America's Roots in the Past: Historical Publication in America to 1860." Unpublished Ph.D. dissertation, Northwestern University, 1967. Useful survey ending with interesting discussion of Bancroft's *History*.
DAWES, N. H., and NICHOLS, F. T. "Revaluing Bancroft," *New*

England Quarterly, VI (1933), 287-93. Balanced assessment of Bancroft as a historian.

HOWE, MARK ANTONY DEWOLFE. *The Life and Letters of George Bancroft*. 2 vols. New York: Scribner's, 1908. Sympathetic account of Bancroft's life with long and useful quotations from his correspondence. Must still be consulted by anyone seriously interested in Bancroft.

KRAUSE, MICHAEL. "George Bancroft, 1834-1934," *New England Quarterly*, VII (1934), 662-86. Centennial assessment of Bancroft as a historian. Stresses his nationalism.

LEVIN, DAVID. *History as Romantic Art*. Stanford, Calif.: Stanford University, 1959. Places Bancroft, Motley, Prescott, and Parkman in the Romantic movement. A model treatment of narrative history as literature.

LEWIS, MERRILL. "Organic Metaphor and Edenic Myth in George Bancroft's *History of the United States*," *Journal of the History of Ideas*, XXVI (1965), 587-92. Stimulating and more sensible than the title suggests.

LOEWENBERG, BERT JAMES. *American History in American Thought*. New York: Simon and Schuster, 1972. Impressive new survey of American historiography. Includes an excellent treatment of Bancroft.

NYE, RUSSEL B. *George Bancroft, Brahmin Rebel*. New York: Knopf, 1944. Standard modern biography of Bancroft, by a distinguished cultural historian. Indispensable.

————— *George Bancroft*. New York: Washington Square Press, 1964. (Great American Thinkers Series.) Rearranges and condenses ideas and materials from Nye's 1944 biography. Has a useful annotated bibliography but does not replace Nye's earlier work.

RATHBUN, JOHN W. "George Bancroft on Man and History," *Transactions of the Wisconsin Academy of Sciences, Arts, and Letters*, XLIII (1954), 51-72. Summarizes Bancroft's philosophy of history.

STEWART, WATT, "George Bancroft," in *Marcus W. Jernegan Essays in American Historiography*, ed. William T. Hutchinson (Chicago: University of Chicago Press, 1937), pp. 1-24. Useful evaluative essay.

VITZTHUM, RICHARD C. "Theme and Method in Bancroft's *History of the United States*," *New England Quarterly*, XLI (1968), 362-80. An excellent treatment of Bancroft's use of sources.

Index